The

JOURNEY
— *to* —
DESTINY

The

JOURNEY

— *to* —

DESTINY

*Discovering
Peace in the Midst
of Any Storm*

SHEILA R. SMITH

WALTON
PUBLISHING HOUSE

Walton Publishing House

Houston, Texas

www.waltonpublishinghouse.com

Printed in the United States of America

ISBN: 978-1-953993-45-8 (Paperback)
ISBN: 978-1-953993-46-5 (Digital/ E-book)

DEDICATION

To my loving husband Dennis, thank you for your love and support through the most trying times of my life.

To my children Sharese, Sheryl, Angel & Ronald, I love you very much and this book is for you.

To every apostle, prophet, intercessor and prayer warrior a million thank-yous for your prayers and support.

CONTENTS

INTRODUCTION

As I began to write this book, I thought about the experiences that shaped me into the woman I am today. I thought about raising my children as a teenage single mother. I thought about the embarrassment of my divorce. I thought about a childhood filled with memories of rejection, loneliness, and abandonment. I thought about how many years hurt, bitterness, and unforgiveness consumed me.

But my story didn't end there.

I also remember when God sent people in my path to give me a word of encouragement or a glimmer of hope. I thought about the prophetic words that came across the pulpit as God sent His prophets to declare life over my future. I also thought about the many times God spoke to me in my dreams, and even in the darkest moments, when everything I loved was turned upside down, He reminded me of His faithfulness.

From this place, I write this book and share the intimate details of my story. From this place, I learned to appreciate the value that I offer to a world of people that God has sent me to minister to. Today I am a witness to the goodness and faithfulness of God as he has blessed me to be a blessing to others. He has called His people to be His hands and feet, and I enjoy doing the work of the Father through my ministry.

My friend, you are not reading this book by accident. This is a divine appointment to help you find your greatness within and see your life from the eyes of a champion. There is so much we need to accomplish for the Kingdom of God, and you my friend, are a part of this uprising of voices of hope.

I am so blessed to connect with you on your road to greatness.

And they overcame him by the blood of the Lamb,
and by the word of their testimony;
and they loved not their lives unto the death.
Revelation 12:11

CHAPTER 1

The Journey to Greatness

Greatness is not measured by what a man or a woman accomplishes, but by the opposition, he or she has overcome to reach their goals."
Dorothy Height

What if I told you that everything you are facing right now is preparation for God's greatness for you? Would you believe me? God has great plans and a purpose for your life. Whether you know it or not, you are on your road to greatness. And although you may not see it now, one day you will understand why you have endured the test and trials of life. I had to come to this realization one day. Finally, after surviving so many of life's obstacles and trials, I realized that there was a winner on the inside of me.

What is the journey to destiny and why it is important that I share it with you? Well, we are all on our journey to destiny. Each of us has a mission that we have been put on earth to accomplish. It's what we were born to do. But it is often a hidden path that few ever find. The journey to destiny is filled with long winding roads, mind-bending twists, and sometimes dead ends. To achieve greatness in our lives, we must be able to overcome challenges, setbacks, and sometimes defeat to reach the destiny God has promised us.

This journey will challenge everything you thought you knew about yourself and cause you to revisit the demons of your past. But if we persevere, we will discover who we are and why we

THE JOURNEY TO DESTINY

were created. Having this understanding will keep you as you travel on the road to greatness. I now understand this process all too well, but it took a while for me to accept this truth. I had questions and I often doubted if things would ever work in my favor. Have you ever experienced a hard time in your life that made you question if God *really* existed? If you're like me, you have asked yourself, why *do so many awful things keep happening in your life? Why do bad things happen to good people, or why is life always full of challenges?* These are questions I used to ask myself daily.

I remember rehearsing those questions in my mind while I drove home from a church service one Sunday. As I contemplated the answer, I started to feel a very strange numbness on my face. The numbness turned into tingling, and then my face felt like it was drooping. *Okay, now what is this? Is this just another one of those trials that I'm getting ready to experience with my health?* I didn't know what was happening, but something wasn't right. I popped a few aspirins sitting in my glove compartment to ease the discomfort and prayed the tingling would stop, but unfortunately, it didn't. So, there I was driving on the highway, alone in my car with no one to call. I became more nervous as I kept driving. The road was dark with barely any lights, and there was no help in sight. Twenty minutes later, I saw an exit off the highway for a convenience store. Desperate to find help, I drove up, jumped out of the car, and started frantically banging on the door.

It was after hours, and the store was closed, but there were still employees working inside. I could see them as I stood outside, desperately waving for someone to come and open the door and help me. I could only imagine what they thought as they watched me outside the glass. They knew something was wrong. I could see the concern on some of their faces, as they looked as if they wanted to open the door to help. Some of the others looked at me as if I were a maniac. I am sure I looked like a madwoman as I stood there pleading for them to help me. After a few minutes, I realized they wouldn't open the door, and I headed back to my car. As I walked, I became more and more disoriented. There were so many thoughts that flooded my mind. *What should I do? Should I call 911? Should I drive myself to the emergency room and take the chance of not making it alive?*

You can't imagine the hopelessness that overtook me. This couldn't have happened at a worse time. The incident occurred during one of the most challenging times in my life. I was homeless and living in Atlanta on my own. Everything I owned was in that car and I couldn't afford to walk away and risk losing it all. More than anything, I feared the police would tow it away and the little possessions I owned would be impounded. This was a test of my faith, so I did the only thing I knew to do, **I prayed**. I cried out loudly to God to save me as I marched around my car, praying my walls down like the children of Jericho. With every march around the car there was a renewed boldness that bolted from my spirit. Something in me wouldn't let me accept that it was the end of my life. Something in me wouldn't let me bow down and became a victim to my life. I thought about the prophetic words that had been spoken over me. I thought about the dreams God had given me, and I knew I couldn't die there. With everything in me, I mustered up a prayer that would touch Heaven.

"Dear Lord, I don't know what is happening to me now, but I do know this one thing. I am your worshiper and I love You, but the dead can't worship You! If I die now, I won't fulfill the things You told me to fulfill.

I kept walking around the car and finally screamed out, "I need you to show me what to do now!"

At that very moment, I received enough strength to get into the car. The Holy Spirit was leading me to drive to the Emergency room, so I did just that. It was another twenty-minute drive, but thankfully I made it to the hospital. When I arrived, I rushed in and told the registrar the symptoms I was experiencing. She immediately admitted me and took me in for an EKG on my heart. I was confused as to why they would do that when I told them about the dropping feeling in my face. They proceeded to run blood tests to determine what was going on. At the end of all the tests, they determined that my body was extremely low in potassium, a 1.9 to be exact. I had no idea what that all meant. They admitted me into the hospital so that they could put potassium back into my body. While having that procedure done, I decided to research on my cell phone the importance of potassium in the human body. I discovered that potassium is an electrolyte and a mineral. It helps keep the water (the amount of fluid inside and outside of the body's cells) and electrolyte balance of the body. It's also important because it helps your nerve's function and muscles contract. Once I read this, I understood why the doctors were in a rush to check my heart. I anxiously waited in the room for my test results.

The nurse returned and said, "With numbers this low, we are confused about why you did not have a heart attack."

I let her in on a secret and I said "I have been dealing with so much lately and have been experiencing debilitating migraines. The only medicine that helps my pain is aspirin. Advil or Tylenol has never worked for me. So, I take 6-8 pills a day. Maybe that is why I'm still here."

The nurse responded, "that sounds like that would be the reason!"

Now let's take a pause here. I know that this sounds very heavy, so I won't go too deep into my story just yet. Much to my surprise, this was only the beginning of the trials I would encounter. I believe that we will experience those moments that test our perseverance on our journey to destiny. When I look back on that time, I can see the hand of God protecting me and keeping the promises He made to me. The road to greatness is filled with windy roads and dead ends, but I believe if we keep on the road, we will discover the beauty that awaits us. If you have ever been on a road trip through the country in the fall, you will see the beauty of the leaves that fall on the ground. If you keep driving, you'll encounter pastures of grass filled with God's beautiful creations. I believe this is what the journey of our lives looks like. The longer we keep on the road, the more we discover the treasures of our lives.

I stand witness that God is fighting for you. And despite the turmoil, He will never leave you or forsake you. He was literally there with me in the middle of it all, and as you read my story, I want you to reflect on the things you have experienced or may be experiencing right now. We all have a journey and a story, but we decide to discover how our experiences define us and shape us into the person we have been created to be.

For the past 30 years, God has had me on assignment to help restore and bring hope to His people. I am a woman of faith and a minister of the Gospel. And my life's purpose is to minister to the hurting people who feel misunderstood by helping the least of these reach their God given purpose. For many years, I have been helping those who were once like I was, who need a helping hand. I have a non-profit ministry that provides clothes, food, and creates many opportunities for me to listen and share God's love. It brings me so much hope as I connect with these families and show them what life can be after their storms. I also love the talks I have with so many people on my journey to help them see life from a perspective of growth and maturity, not from a victim's perspective in life. I teach them how to release the pain and hurt that others have caused them

In this book, I will be sharing a few lessons that I have learned throughout my life. The first lesson is to release the offense and victim mentality. We must be willing to quickly forgive others, release any hurt, and not hold on to offense. If we do, the offense will always turn to bitterness and hatred in our lives resulting in some type of physical illness. This, too I have experienced, battled, and finally overcame.

I have learned to take the time to reflect on the experiences of my life and process the lesson. This means that instead of being a victim, we can use the experiences of our journey as fuel for our next level. This is often easier said than done, but this is where we must rely on God's strength to help carry us through.

Many of you reading this book are on your journey to destiny. I believe that you picked up this book to help shift the trajectory of your life. Like many people, you have experienced some ordeals that have caused you to doubt if you will ever reach the finish line. However, I'm assuring you that all your experiences are for good, and you'll understand better if you can look at your struggles from a champion's perspective. On the road to greatness, you will experience setbacks and trials, but in everything, you must not give up. I can assure you that if you keep going and don't give up, you will see the beauty of your life be revealed.

As I share my story with you, I want you to think about where you are today and where you see yourself going. I want you to think about God's promises to you. Hold those close to your heart and never give up. One of the things that I love about my relationship with God is that He constantly keeps me on the path to becoming who He has called me to be. Even though there are times when I get off track, His mercy and grace always bring me back to Him. When I look at some of the great men and women of the Bible, I understand how He uses the foolish things to confound the wise. I also love when He tells us in His Word that all things, no matter how dark or ugly they may be, it all works together for our good. So, in all your pain and struggles, never forget that everything works for your good.

"And we know that all things work together for good to them that love God, to them who are called according to his purpose."

Romans 8:28 KJV

I wrote this book with you in mind. In fact, the Holy Spirit divinely inspired this book to help reveal the truth of your story and how you are right where you are supposed to be. There are so many things I want to show you that the Holy Spirit has taught me throughout my life. I could have become bitter, or I could change my perspective on how my story will help impact the lives of many others. I chose the latter, and as you continue to read, you will understand why I feel this way. I'm using my story and testimony because I know what it's like to be without and a person who needs help. I know what it's like to feel shame, embarrassment, guilt, and sometimes regret. But I can thankfully say that God uses my life as a vessel to help others. While I didn't always receive the help I needed, God chose to give me a ministry that helps families. I believe that was all a part of what God had planned for me. Taking me through while teaching me the strength of who I am.

CHAPTER 2

Remember Where You Come From

For I know the plans I have for you, declares the Lord, plans to prosper you and not to harm you, plans to give you hope and a future.

Jeremiah 29:11

I have often heard it's not about how you start but how you finish. As I reflect on my life, I understand this statement more and more. Growing up with a silver spoon in my mouth would have been the ideal situation. That, however, was not the case for me. I was born and raised in New Jersey in a time when racial equality looked nothing like it looks today. Even today, it could stand to be much better, but there is a world of difference compared to back then. We lived in a reasonably large city neighborhood, but it still had the small town feel. We had the luxury of living five minutes from the beach. That was a joy and a privilege.

Back in the '70s, the sky seemed so much bluer, and the flowers gave out so much more fragrance. Times were different and simpler. Things on television were not vulgar and nasty. Parents did not have to race to switch the channels before we could see something that our little eyes had no business seeing. In my house, we could only get two radio stations; a channel that played cowboy music and one that played Pop and Folk music, and all was well in our world.

Our family grew up on the wrong side of the tracks. We lived in the projects, and my father died when I was four years old.

As a result, my mom became a young widow. Shortly after his death, she decided that it would be best for us to move in with our grandmother. My mom had to work two jobs to care for my sister, grandmother, and me. She rode public transportation to and from her jobs every day. She did what she needed to do to take care of our family. The workload was stressful for her and was very hard on her physically, but it didn't stop her. Her work ethic was impeccable. I have never witnessed anything like it in my life. Seeing her do that for us drove me to keep her and all her kind acts stored deep in my mind. It was a good thing I did because it helped me in the future.

The apartment where we lived was rather large. It had four bedrooms. However, we had enough stuff in there to fill a six-bedroom house. To accurately describe it, I would have to say that it reminds me of "Sanford and Son." It was horrible. I hated and despised living there. I felt so out of place, and I knew that I did not belong there.

The apartment consisted of piles and piles of useless junk, old papers, old clothes, and broken furniture; you name it, we had it. Because the housekeeping was very poor, it caused the mouse and roach population to flourish. The rule of thumb is that roaches come out mainly at night. If you see one out during the day, you have an infestation. That went for rats and mice as well. Our roaches and mice dwelled openly among us in the daytime.

Often, I looked around silently observing my family members. I could not understand why this environment didn't seem to bother anyone else but me. I hated being there and many times, the thought of having to return their daily made me literally sick to my stomach. It was filthy and disgusting in every single corner of the house.

My sister and I always had to share a bedroom. Three other bedrooms were available, but we had to share the rooms because our apartment was a community house. When other family members were evicted from their homes, they would bring their family to "Grandma's" house (our house) to live until they got back on their feet. It was very uncomfortable because the apartment was never kept clean and adding large amounts of people to the equation made it worse. With so many people in the house, there was truly no reason for the apartment to be in its usual state of disgust. I was tired of it, but I had no say in what was done there.

Growing up, I was always an extremely shy girl. After my father passed away, there were no male figures in my life after his death. My mom did not want to bring a man into her life and take the chance of him raping or molesting us. She sacrificed her life to keep us safe. She went without the love of a man for the remainder of her days, which really made me sad for her. Even though I knew why I knew that she was lonely, she would sit on the couch and look out of the window, and one single tear would roll down her face. She had to be strong for the family. A lot of people depended on her. Not only my siblings and I, but everyone also relied on her. She was the pillar of our entire family. My mother was strong and independent, and she protected us as best as she could. I applaud my mother for the sacrifices she made for my sister and me.

Looking for Love

A father figure is paramount for every child, especially girls. Not being able to look up to a male figure in life, or having affirmation from a man, leads to a girl making poor choices, mainly in relationships. "Countless studies have shown that fatherlessness has an extremely negative impact on a girls' self-esteem. Her confidence in her abilities and value as a human being can be significantly diminished if her father or a father figure isn't there. Academically, personally, professionally, physically, socially, and romantically, a woman's self-esteem is diminished in every setting if she did not form a healthy relationship with her father."[1]

Being a young girl looking for love, I met a popular young boy at school who the other girls also admired. His name was CB. I thought he was a good boy because he seemed to really like me and treated me like a young lady. I also liked the fact that although my friends were sleeping around at a young age, he didn't pressure me to have sex with him. CB and I had the best time when we were together. We were young, and just sitting and holding hands and laughing with him gave me comfort. He was my very first boyfriend. Being with him took my mind off the madness that was going on in my home life.

After some time, my infatuation for him grew and before long the "no sex" talks shifted to him influencing me to do something I knew I wasn't ready to do. While talking to him one day, he

---

1   Mckenna Meyers, "Fatherless Daughters: How Growing Up Without a Dad Affects Women." We Have Kids, March 7, 2022, https://wehavekids.com/family-relationships/When-Daddy-Dont-Love-Their-Daughters-What-Happens-to-Women-Whose-Fathers-Werent-There-for-Them

made it clear that he only dealt with girls that were virgins. I proudly announced that I was a virgin and wasn't interested in sex; I didn't know what else to do. I didn't want to lose CB, so I went along with the idea. I was naive, but the only thing that was going on in my mind was being able to get out of that crazy house into the arms of someone who would love me. That to me, was the most exciting thought that I had ever had in my entire young life.

During the two weeks of talking, he said he wanted me to be his girlfriend. I agreed to that simply because I had no one else asking me to be their girl, so this felt very good to me. This also helped my self-esteem after what happened with the other joker that had previously cheated on me. This was the surefire way to put that situation behind me thoroughly. While he defined what a girlfriend for him would be, he let me know that there would be sex involved. I was quiet when he mentioned that because I wasn't too excited about that part. I was a virgin, and naturally, I really didn't know what to expect. I didn't want to engage in sex. I only wanted to be loved and held. I knew that I was not going to get what I desired without giving him what he wanted, so I figured that would be the price that I would have to pay to receive the love I needed. I agreed and I became CB's girlfriend and did what was necessary to make him happy.

My Mother's Dream

One day as I was washing clothes in the laundry room, I heard Mom's voice downstairs. It was so early that I had to look at my watch to check the time. I yelled downstairs to say "hi" to her.

She walked upstairs to talk to me. Unfortunately, she didn't look like her usual happy self. I stopped washing and asked her what was wrong? She made the statement that that shifted my world. "Sheila, last night I dreamed that you were pregnant. Please do not kill my grandchild."

I was in a state of shock and lied and told myself that I was not doing anything! Then I just became very quiet. By this time, I had not heard from CB in 5 months. My mind raced with all kinds of different thoughts. I was in total denial of being pregnant because I only had sex one time and there was no way that I could possibly be pregnant. I was only 15 years old! But I couldn't shake the fear of being pregnant. Whenever my mother had dreamed or announced that someone was expecting a baby, it was always proven to be true. *Could this be happening to me?* I wondered. I kept trying to convince myself that she was wrong. I was still skinny, and my body was not showing any signs of pregnancy. I was so confused. I toggled between being pregnant and becoming a mother. One minute I was hoping I wasn't pregnant, and the next I was thinking that having a baby may be a good thing because I would have someone to love, and they would love me in return. A part of me was excited about that.

A month went by, and I started noticing a change in my body. My once flat chest had form. I still wasn't ready to accept the truth that I was pregnant. I decided not to dwell on the pregnancy thoughts, so I read and studied like never before. I was trying to do anything to keep my mind off it. It did not work. I was consumed with wanting to know for sure. I finally built up the courage to ask my mother to take me to the doctor so that I could be tested to know once and for all if I was pregnant. My mother worked for a Jewish doctor who had a good friend who was an OB-GYN. She made an appointment and took me to the doctor for a pregnancy test. There weren't instant test results during those times, so I had to wait three days to receive the news. Those next few days were the longest three days of my life. Day three finally arrived and the nurse called my mother on her job. She held the news and waited to get off work to give me the message in person.

That day she walked through the door looking very normal and happy. She called me into the kitchen and said "The doctor's office called me today. You are pregnant. I will say this to you again. Please don't kill my only grandchild. Promise me."

I just stared off into space. *Was this really happening to me?* I wasn't ready to become a mother. I had given up my virginity, and now at just 15, I was pregnant. It was the last thing I thought would have ever happened to me. I had such a bright future ahead. The news put me in a state of shock. I stood there unable to move or say anything. No words would come out of my mouth. I felt like I was in the twilight zone. This could not be happening to me. A week went by, and I went back and forth in my mind about telling CB that I was pregnant. Finally, I talked myself into calling him and decided to tell him that I was pregnant, and we needed to discuss a plan moving forward. His response was insensitive and struck me at my core. The first question out of his mouth was,

"Is it mine?"

I had never in my life been so angry. *What was he trying to imply? Was he insinuating that I was just having free will sex with anyone?* I couldn't believe that he thought of me in that light. Then, after a slight pause, his response to me was, "Well, you know what to do; have an abortion." His words further dumbfounded the initial shock I had about my pregnancy. *How could this be happening to me?*

I felt as if my whole world was caving in on me. I was not too fond of the idea of having an abortion. But I didn't feel as if there was any other choice. I was embarrassed by getting pregnant, and I entertained the idea. I thought it would be a good way to cover up my mistake. CB said that if I did not have the abortion, he would want nothing to do with me. In my young mind, that would destroy what little family we were building, and I did not want to do that, so I agreed and went to a place that would do the abortion in Newark, NJ.

After I agreed to the abortion, CB suggested that we go together. I am sure that was his way of ensuring that I went through with it. So, on the day of the appointment, we met up and rode the train to Newark because I was too far along for the clinics in my local area to perform the procedure. When we arrived at the clinic, the nurse escorted me in to have the abortion. As I was putting on my surgical gown for the procedure, I clearly heard my mother's voice. I put on the gown and as I was laying on the cold metal table, I heard her voice again.

"Sheila, please do not kill my grandchild."

I sat up on the table and I heard it yet again. "Do not kill my grandchild."

There were so many emotions and thoughts running through my mind. Before I knew it, I had jumped up from the table and put my clothes back on before the doctor came in, and I rushed out of the building. I couldn't go through with it. I couldn't let my mother down. She had sacrificed so much for me; the least I could do was give her what she asked for. When I walked out, my boyfriend saw that I was still pregnant and was very upset with me. He kept his promise and true to form, the relationship didn't last, and we decided to part ways. I was sad but I felt I made the right decision by keeping my baby.

Teenage Motherhood

I was now 16 years old and would be a mother. My life literally flashed before my eyes. The part that hurt me the most was knowing how people would view me as a promiscuous girl, and that simply was not the case. I had sex one time and became pregnant. Many people wouldn't believe it, but I was a proven case study. I would not have believed it either had someone walked up to me or told me that it only takes once.

I endured the pregnancy and tried my best to not allow others' opinions to affect me. Every day I woke up and went to school and attempted to keep my life as normal as I could with the situation I was facing. I was going to love my baby and be the best mother I could. Nine months came so quickly, and it was time to have my baby. The labor was intensive, lasting for a total of 28 hours but it was all worth it when I laid my eyes on her. When my daughter was born, she was the loveliest little girl. I was stunned at how she looked exactly like my baby pictures. I immediately thought to myself, "This is what I almost missed." She was a very good baby too. Not too much crying and easily satisfied. Baby Sarah was better than I had imagined she would be. She became my first glimpse of what love looked like.

After I had the baby, my mother took me to get on birth control. I faithfully took birth control because I knew I wasn't prepared to have another child and wanted to graduate high school. But as fate would have it, the birth control didn't work, and I got pregnant two more times at ages 17 and18. I felt I had ruined my life. I was a teenage mother trying to finish high school and life was a major struggle. I could barely sleep at night and was ready to give up on my dreams. I felt like my life was ending and I would never be able to amount to anything.

How could this be happening to me? I constantly questioned. *I am on birth control, but I am still getting pregnant. How is this my fault?*

I did not accept responsibility for the role I played in becoming pregnant with my three kids. Not acknowledging the part I had to play, kept me in a repetitive cycle that I was not in any way prepared for.

Raising My Children

As a teenage mother, I remember how hard it was to raise my children. Reflecting on that day on the surgical table, I can honestly say that I am happy that I had them earlier in my life. I am so glad that I chose to keep my babies, although I was afraid and often didn't know what I was doing. My children and I grew up together. Being a mother made me mature quickly. I had to learn everything fast. You can say it was on the job training. Having my babies helped me to become quick on my toes and adapt very quickly to change. I became a survivor and learned how to make better choices.

I loved my children with all my heart. I didn't have much but I wanted to give them a safe environment. Spending time with them was essential. I was still living with my mom at my grandmother's house, and I was thankful for the support my mom gave me. But we started to grow out of the space, and I knew I needed to provide more for my children.

I laugh now when I think about it, but I wanted to become a TV mom, providing the essentials they needed and creating that picture perfect home. I did everything I could to provide a stable environment. I made sure that their clothes were clean. I taught them the alphabet. I cooked them healthy meals just like the ones I watched on the Brady Bunch. I always thought that having a routine helped with stability. I made sure they went to bed at a decent hour and put them on a schedule. Having children required me to become resourceful and to think on my feet. There was no room for wasting time and I had to learn how to survive fast. I didn't have the luxury of being a kid anymore. I had to grow up. I learned a little bit of everything so that people wouldn't outsmart me because I knew that I had to survive not only now for myself but for them. I also had to make better choices.

THE JOURNEY TO DESTINY

One of the things that bothered me the most was raising my children without a father. I knew its effect on me and how it affected my decisions. But I didn't want that to be our family story. So, I prayed and asked God to send me someone that would love my children the way I did. Until He sent someone, I remained single and raised them the best way I knew how, just like my mom did.

CHAPTER 3

Is That You God?

My sheep listen to my voice; I know them,
and they follow me. I give them eternal life,
and they shall never perish; no one will
snatch them out of my hand.
John 10:27-28

I was introduced to God at a young age. Growing up, my mother took the time to teach us Bible verses, and she made sure we knew who Jesus was. Although we were young, she planted a seed in my heart that I would never forget. She told us her testimony about how God healed her from different things in her body. When she was a young girl, God healed her from a very acute case of stuttering. Listening to her, you would never know she stuttered. She was the most articulate woman I have ever heard, even though she only had a sixth-grade education. Mom had to end her education early to help raise eleven of her brothers and sisters.

She stressed the importance of reading and knowing the Bible. She would pull the Bible out and make us sit next to her while she read to us. She would say, "Girls, if you are ever in trouble, read Psalm 91," and then she would read it to us. She went further on to say,

"If you ever need God to help you no matter what it is, then read Psalm 23 and Psalm 121." God is always listening to you when you call, my mom reassured us.

I learned about faith from my mother. My mom had a powerful testimony about how she constantly wanted to have children but had challenges conceiving. The doctors told her for years that she couldn't bear children. My mom stretched her faith and prayed constantly for years, but nothing happened. Then one day, after many attempts, she wasn't feeling well and decided to go to the doctor. That's when she found out that she was pregnant with me. She called me her miracle baby. She said I was an absolute miracle, and she knew I was special. After I was born, they diagnosed me with tuberculosis, but even that couldn't shake her faith. She prayed again and God healed me. Her testimonies increased my faith at a very young age.

I would continue to learn lessons about God that were simple yet profound. One very windy day, while we were stuck inside the house, we decided to play upstairs. Grandma called me downstairs to get her a glass of water and I brought it to her.

She said, "Look out the window. Do you see the trees swaying back and forth?"

"Yes, I see them," I answered,

She replied, "That is the trees praising the Lord."

"Really?" I questioned.

"Yes," she said. "Everything must praise the Lord. If we don't praise the Lord, even the rocks will cry out."

I just looked at her because it didn't make sense that the rocks would cry out. How in the world can rocks cry out? Not fully understanding the statement my grandmother made, I went back upstairs to play with the other kids.

God showed up in the everyday things of life, letting me know He was there. After that, I began to have more encounters. On another occasion, at about 2:00 am my grandma called me downstairs on a Friday night. We had many cousins staying in the house with us at that time, and out of everyone, she called me downstairs to look at the preacher on TV. I wondered why, with a house full of kids, why did she call only me? As I watched this preacher on TV, he talked about tithes and offerings. I didn't understand why the preacher was asking poor people like us for money on TV. He was wearing a nice suit, and he looked rich. Everything about him screamed money. I was annoyed and questioned my grandmother about this. She explained that tithing is our obligation to God. The ten percent is the tithe, and the extra is the offering.

The preacher also said that if you have a need, act in faith towards your need, sow a seed and God would meet whatever needs that you may have. When the show was over, I shrugged it off and went back upstairs to sleep, still not fully understanding why she called only me.

The message didn't resonate with me then, but I stored all this information in the back of my mind until I was an adult and mature enough to apply the principles, I heard that night. The seed for sowing and reaping was planted inside of me; although it took years to manifest, the word of God would not return void.

"Bring the whole tithe into the storehouse, that there may be food in my house. Test me in this," says the LORD Almighty, "and see if I will not throw open the floodgates of heaven and pour out so much blessing that you will not have room enough for it".

Malachi 3:10 NIV

Testing My Faith

When I was about 19 years old, I started putting this "faith" information to use. There was a time when I had a lot of needs, so I decided to see if there was any truth to what the preacher said. I needed a car badly to transport myself and my children. I didn't know what to do, so I prayed and was led to reach out to the TV evangelist. I sent my first tithe to his ministry. He told the tithers that if we wanted a car, to sweep out the driveway in faith and speak to the driveway to get ready for a car. I did as he instructed for about two weeks, and guess what! I received my first car. This was the first encounter I would have with a prophetic voice. I was so excited to receive my car, and I wondered what else I could speak into my life by faith.

"And my God shall supply all your needs according to His riches in glory by Christ Jesus."

Philippians 4:19 NIV

That started my faith journey, and I knew that God and His promises were real. I also began to respect the voice of God's prophets. I would later learn that prophets are mouthpieces for God that He trusts to speak the things they hear Him speaking.

After that day, there were so many times where the principle of supernatural blessings manifested because I learned and applied the law of sowing and reaping. I used this same principle when I needed an apartment. And honestly, I've lost count of the things God has helped me with because this has been proven in my life repeatedly.

Receiving The Holy Spirit

Years later, I would receive the Holy Spirit and be empowered to do more for God. Even when the right people didn't necessarily surround me, God showed me His hand was on my life. People around me started to notice the change. The things I was once comfortable doing, the Holy Spirit convicted me to stop.

I was in a relationship with a young man with whom I would smoke marijuana. One day, after a quick stop at the local drugstore, he asked me to light one up for him. At the time, I wasn't sure what came over me, but I asked him if he could do it himself. He did and passed the marijuana over to me. Reluctantly as I was taking it out of his hand, I heard a loud audible voice say, "You don't need that." I looked in the back seat because that was where the voice was coming from. I had to stop and think if anyone was sitting back there because the voice was so clear. I wasn't under the influence of any drugs or alcohol that day, and my mind was clear, but I just chalked it up to me hearing things.

Finally, I decided to hand the joint back to him. He handed it back to me a minute later and said, "Hit it!"

Then I heard the voice again, but this time even louder and clearer. "You don't need that!" I finally said to him, "I don't need that." He began to blow smoke in my face as a temptation and I simply said to myself, "I must really not need it after all." It was so strange because I had no desire to smoke with him.

Days went by and I had not even thought about the fact that I had gone five days without taking a hit. I was an everyday weed smoker, but I had no urges, cravings, or desires for it. I was truly delivered. It stunned me, and I was so excited about God's changes in me.

That incident caused me to rededicate my life back to Christ. I started listening to my church music again as I used to when I was having hard times throughout my life. I started watching Christian television as I used to when living at home. I even found the same man on TV that my grandma called me downstairs to watch in the middle of the night. I felt so much peace. I had never felt like this in my entire life. I decided to go after this God that I heard my mom and grandma talk about. I wanted to find out if He was real for me. I knew He was real because He took away my desire to smoke drugs. That was a miracle because I loved to smoke and to have no desire proved to me that there must be a real God.

After being set free from doing all types of different drugs, things became clearer for me. I decided that I needed to know more about this God that so easily delivered me from drugs. While I started looking for ways to learn about this God, I remembered what the man said that I met in the laundromat a few years back. He said that I needed to accept the Lord into my life and my heart to make it into Heaven.

One day, as I watched a Christian television program, they asked if anyone wanted salvation, and if they want a relationship with the Lord. I thought *this is my chance to get it right with God.* I had done so many wrong things, I wasn't sure if He could forgive someone like me, but that preacher said that no matter what I had done in the past, God's loving, open arms were available to me right then. I decided to take him up on his offer and I did it. I became "Born Again." The funny thing is, I didn't feel any different. That preacher warned me that I might not feel any different, but I must believe that the price had been paid, and I must have faith and know that I had been redeemed.

From that day I read the Bible and bought tapes of the Bible. I really wanted to learn as much as possible. I felt the pull to know more about Jesus. And since I was going to be a Christian now, it was even more important for my growth. I would flip through the channels looking at different television shows in hopes to find something that would appeal to me. I wanted something that was not a lot of hollering, but I also did not want anything to bore me either. One day, I saw one of the same pastors that my grandmother used to watch on TV. I watched him for about 15 minutes and suddenly, he started singing in an unknown tongue.

When we were children, we would play when church was on pretending that we were speaking in tongues. Grandma would say, "Keep on playing you're going to catch them for real." Of course, we did not care nor didn't pay attention to any of that. My mind flashed back to that very day when that pastor was singing in tongues. I listened to the heavenly language, and it was like that song was etched in my mind. I would look at other television programs and they would mail out little booklets on salvation and how to receive the Lord as your personal Savior. On this particular day, they were offering a pamphlet on how to receive the Holy Spirit. I was so excited because that was what I needed. I needed to learn what this whole thing was about. The whole ordeal sounded a little bit frightening to be honest, but I needed to know more. Something in me desired to dig deeper to find out more.

Some weeks later, I received the book in the mail and read it from cover to cover. I even re-read it several times to ensure that I fully understood the entire book. Basically, receiving the Holy Spirit was just like receiving salvation. It was a free gift and all I had to do was to simply receive it. That was easier said than done. I did not know how to receive anything. I always had to fight and war for everything that I had. I didn't get the meaning of just receiving it. I had been to churches previously where we tarried on the altar waiting for the Holy Spirit, but I could never seem to receive Him. Other people got up from the altar speaking in tongues, not me. I didn't understand what I was doing wrong. I became very frustrated about that, so I never bothered again, until then. I was told that the Holy Spirit was the power to help you to live this Christian life. The Holy Spirit is a teacher, comforter, and helper. I also learned that the Holy Spirit is a personality and not a thing.

I decided that I must have it, and I didn't want to give up this time until I received Him. I decided to sing songs and worship the Lord. I sang the same songs that I saw the preacher sing on TV when he was singing in tongues. I even mimicked his tongues. I literally sang the song note for note. I yearned and desired for the Holy Spirit. I talked to the Lord and told Him that I wanted to be filled with the Holy Spirit. I kept on forging and being hungry for the Holy Spirit. This was not a one-day process. I did this for hours every day for a week straight. Then, on the seventh day, something different happened, unlike any of the other days.

Encounter with the Holy Spirit

I couldn't put my finger on what was different. It was just that the atmosphere was unusual in the room. I had been using my bedroom as my prayer room, and after I had dropped the children off at school, I went into my prayer room to pray for the Holy Ghost, and within 20 minutes, it hit me. I could not stop talking in tongues for five hours when it fell on me. I knew that day God was real, and there was more to Him than I ever knew. That was my first encounter with the Holy Spirit.

"For as many as are led by the Spirit of God, these are
sons of God".

Romans 8:14

I had to stop just long enough to pick the children up from
school. It was the strangest yet not the least bit scary thing I had
ever experienced. I thought that it would be scary, but it wasn't.
I believe that's why it took me so long to receive. After receiving
Him, I knew that the problem was me all along. Fear had gripped
me and kept me from receiving what belonged to me.

Many new Christians don't know that they have access to the
Holy Spirit when they become born again. The Holy Spirit is
there to help us, but we must be open to allow Him. The Holy
Spirit is real and wants to help us in every phase and area.

That night when I picked up my friend from work, I was so
excited to share with him my experience of receiving the Holy
Spirit, but I decided not to. He came from a Muslim background,
and he really didn't understand Christianity, so I just kept it to
myself. He had already been annoyed because of my lifestyle
changes anyway. I didn't want to push him any further over the
edge. I didn't try to change his ways because I had recently come
out of the same lifestyle; how dare I try to change him? I just
decided to let him see that I had changed for real, and maybe in
seeing that, he would change as I had.

Once I received the Holy Spirit my eyes opened to a lot of
things. He taught me a lot of things. The major thing was that
I was living with a man that was not my husband. That really

concerned me because sin grieves the Holy Spirit. I knew that I shouldn't be doing that, and I began to feel bad. I wanted to do things the right way. I told my boyfriend about my recent encounters with God and how I felt about our lifestyle. He didn't want me to compromise my values, so he agreed to marry me officially. I was glad that I was able to obey and do the thing that pleased God.

CHAPTER 4

Experiencing Loss: The Road to Sorrow

For he has not despised or scorned the suffering of the afflicted one; he has not hidden his face from him but has listened to his cry for help.

Psalms 22:24 NIV

married my high school sweetheart at twenty years old and gladly moved out of my grandmother's house. I was so excited to begin that new life. My children were under five years old, and I would finally be able to give them the life they deserved. I would be able to offer them a home where I would be more in control of who visited and how clean the home would be. I hated being in my grandmother's house with so many people coming and going where the standard of living was so low. More than anything, I wanted to give them a loving and stable home environment. I wanted to provide them with a 2-parent household. That was something I did not have growing up.

The fairytale quickly ended during the first years of marriage. Although we tried our best to make it work, things were a struggle. As a young family, we had many financial issues. To make matters worse, I didn't feel welcomed by his family. However, I was determined not to let those problems take us out. I was a prayer warrior, and I started to pray more during that time and seek God. I wanted to be a good wife and mother and do things God's way.

One day I was invited to a church by a coworker. My family and I accepted the invitation. This church was just what we needed.

After the visit we fell in love with the church and joined after visiting in just a few short weeks. The worship and the preaching were great. It really made a difference in our lives. Being involved in church life gave me the strength and the hope that whatever we encountered in life, we would be able to get through it since God and our new church were in our life. We took things day by day. Some days were easier than others. Nevertheless, we made it through and felt that God had our backs. However, after a few years of having this great optimism, things started to fall apart.

It wasn't long before the struggles in our marriage intensified, and my idea of the perfect life and marriage came crashing down. It wasn't all at once, but over the years, while serving in ministry, I realized that some things that were preached didn't align with my spirit. My husband and I stopped agreeing on many things, and before long, our marriage began to deteriorate. I thought being active in church with my family would protect us from the enemy's attacks. I thought that when you do things God's way, things always work out. I was wrong. But the more I prayed, the more my husband and I began to pull away from each other.

The journey to destiny placed me face to face with disappointment and hurt. Our home was in an uproar which made it difficult for me to function at work. It was so devastating and embarrassing to watch my marriage crumble because I had witnessed to many people about my relationship with Christ. I had served tirelessly in ministry and did whatever it took to walk with Christ, but here I was faced with a messy divorce and the reality that I would be a single mother *again.*

It was an ugly split. Friends became foes as people picked their sides as to which spouse, they would continue to be friends with. I don't know if I had ever felt that level of loneliness before. The people I had shared intimate moments with, prayed for in their times of need, and fellowshipped with, quickly left my side. It seemed as if everyone was against me. The pastor took my ex-husband's side because they were friends and because he felt men needed to stick together. I was becoming numb to it all as I watched my world spin out of control.

While I was going through the divorce, the unthinkable happened. My mother, who had been my rock and my supporter, passed away and a month later, I lost my grandmother. It was the worst time of my life. My matriarchs, my pillars, were now gone. My foundation was shaken at the core. I wondered why God was allowing this to happen to me. I felt weak and depressed. I couldn't be there for my children as my heart ached so baldly. *God, how much more can I take?*

Having to deal with all the loss, I also realized I had lost my entire church family. One of the members secretly shared that the others were prohibited from speaking with me. I had been ostracized and they were not allowed to have any communication with me. They would no longer be allowed back at the church if they did. I honestly thought she was making up a farfetched story. I had been a pillar member of the church, served faithfully and for many years, and was a faithful giver. I refused to believe that I could be treated like that after dedicating my life to the work of that ministry.

Her story was confirmed one day while I was outside taking care of the lawn. I must say that this was new for me. My husband had moved out and now I was responsible for the yard work. I could no longer afford a landscaper while going through my divorce. While cutting my grass, I saw a male church member riding down my street. My street was a popular road, and it was easy to see the people as they drove by. When this gentleman drove by, he didn't wave hello or stop to offer help. It was then that I knew what she had stated was true. I was devastated. I lay in the grass of my front yard and cried. I had lost so much in a matter of two months that I thought that would lose my mind.

I wanted to have the support of my church family, but they turned their backs on me during one of the loneliest times of my life. I felt betrayed. I needed to find a safe place to release all the pain I was experiencing. Looking back on those times, I realize God allowed me to be isolated because He wanted me to connect with Him. However, I began to pull further away instead of pulling toward God. I had so many more questions about what I was experiencing, but few answers

Isolation for Your Calling

When God is working on you, He may require you to isolate yourself from people and consecrate you. There are many examples in the Bible where God separated people from their familiar comforts to be connected to Him. Abraham, David, Moses and even Jesus Christ had to undergo this phase. And although isolation came with pain, it was an essential part of the journey.

My employer knew that I was going through a lot at home and suggested that I speak to a therapist to help me sort everything out, so I did. I did not feel that I was mentally stable because I was experiencing all the major losses simultaneously. The doctor wanted to put me on a handful of medicines for depression. The medication made me feel like I was another person. It affected how I functioned, and I didn't like how it made me feel. I could not take that medicine, or I would not be able to perform my job. I had to cope the best way that I knew how. I felt like I was barely surviving going on autopilot. That was all I had at the time.

My Spiritual Weapon

The spiritual weapon to help me get through the perils of life has always been my singing. As I sang and worshiped, it would lift my spirit. In worship, I connect with God and express my love for Him. I had always been in singing groups, on worship teams, and in choirs. Singing and worshiping the Lord brought me great peace and joy. So, I decided to use that as my medicine. Needless to say, it was beginning to work.

One day I noticed that I kept having bad sinus headaches. Someone at work informed me that more than half of the ladies on my floor were experiencing similar symptoms, and many of them were having sinus surgery. I was concerned so I decided to go to an ear, nose, and throat doctor and Otolaryngologist. At the appointment, the doctor put the scope into my nose and throat. What he discovered shocked me. He found polyps on my vocal cords and advised that I had a deviated septum. I asked him what I should do. He seemed a bit rushed and quickly advised me that I needed surgery. I didn't seek another opinion, nor did I question his diagnosis, and I was immediately led into surgery. After I came out, I was free from the sinus headaches I had experienced for years.

A few months later, as I was singing one of my favorite songs, I struggled to hit the soprano notes that I once sang so effortlessly. I knew there was a recovery time from the surgery, so I decided to give myself a little more time to recover. More weeks went by, and singing was still a struggle. After doing some research, I found the surgery had damaged my vocal cords. I couldn't believe I had yet another blow. I became even more upset with God. My voice was what I used to sing praises, but it also was what put a smile on my face despite everything I was struggling with. I questioned God.

One thing I also lost and did not realize until months later was my ability to be able to sing anymore. I was devastated because I believed my voice was what connected me to God in worship during that time. That was another difficult blow to me. Yes, I could still worship, but now it would have to be alone with God. I loved singing in the choir and worshiping with others at church. I wondered why. Why would something so precious be so easily taken from me? I was upset with God for not warning me or giving me the wisdom not to have the procedure done. I was upset with the doctor. Surely, he could have warned me of the possible effects of the surgery. I was upset with the world, and I was losing everyone and everything that mattered to me in my life.

Loss of my marriage...

Loss of my mother...

Loss of my grandmother...

Loss of my singing voice...

My mind started wondering about the next bad thing that would happen in my life. My goodness! I was so mad, angry, and bitter that the God I had served for so many years would turn His back on me and watch me struggle in every area of my life. *Why me God? What did I do to deserve such pain?*

"My brethren, count it all joy when you fall into various trials, knowing that the testing of your faith produces patience. But let patience have its perfect work, that you may be perfect and complete, lacking nothing".

James 1:2-4 NKJV

CHAPTER 5

The Big Move

If your world doesn't allow you to dream,
move to one where you can."
Billy Idol

needed a fresh start, and after much contemplation, I made a major life decision to move to Atlanta. The cost of living was much cheaper than in New Jersey, but I was happy about starting over more than that. I felt that with this big move, I would be able to recreate myself, meet a good group of people, and leave the pain of my past behind me. So, I moved to Atlanta Georgia, with very few of my things and a few pieces of furniture and other household items.

During that time, Atlanta was booming, and it was the place for black professionals to connect and bloom in their careers. Some of my friends lived there and constantly hyped the city, the sites, and the social scene to me. But truthfully, they didn't have to sell me on the idea I wanted to get as far from New Jersey and the people that lived there as quickly as possible.

There wasn't as much of a culture shock as I thought. New Jersey is the Garden State. We are primarily rural land filled with farmland, cows, and horses. The environment looked exactly like Georgia. I loved the south because I wanted a laid-back life, which is vastly different from the rat race I grew up in. I looked forward to learning about the culture. The first thing on my agenda was finding a pizza spot that closely resembled New

York style pizza. Although I never found that spot, I had found a place that felt like home to me for the first time. Even today, no matter where I am in the world, I will always consider the Atlanta metropolitan area my home.

I took the risk to move on a wing and a prayer. When I moved to Georgia, I didn't have a job, and I threw caution to the wind. The one thing that I did to prepare on the way there was to get an apartment. Before leaving New Jersey, I found an apartment in a town called Sandy Springs. I had no idea about the town itself, but I figured I would learn all about it upon arrival. Atlanta was much busier than anticipated. I was surprised by the hustle and bustle and was shocked to see just how busy the roads and the area were especially after moving from a little town without any real traffic. Atlanta was intimidating to me because it was so big, and the people drove like maniacs. I learned that the reason for the scary driving is because Atlanta has people literally from all over the country. It's a big melting pot of drivers from everywhere trying to navigate the interstates, and it would take some getting used to live there and thrive.

Culture

My Jersey roots became even more pronounced as I met people in the deep south. The people in Georgia were completely different. We ate differently. We spoke differently. We even expressed ourselves differently in New Jersey. It wasn't long before this loud talking, hand motioning, and straight shooter woman would have to taper back the big personality a bit. I remember when I first realized that people were taking offense to how I spoke to them. I knew from that day that I would quickly have to change. I had to constantly remind myself that it was the south.

One of the greatest differences that I loved the most in Atlanta, was the cost of living. It was almost three times less expensive than New Jersey. Everything was cheaper: the apartments, the utilities, and the food. I was so surprised how far I could stretch my tiny budget, which was ideal for a person who was starting from scratch. I was convinced that I would have a great life there, but also had to consider that the jobs would not pay like they paid up north with a cheaper cost of living.

I started my job search, and almost immediately, landed a job at a staffing agency as an assistant manager. The job was great and exciting. It required me to visit different staffing agencies, build relationships with the existing account contacts, and ensure that the employees were doing a good job. I enjoyed it so much. I held that job for three years until the agency closed its doors. After finally getting established in the area, working for several years, and being ready to put down roots, I was laid off. There were a lot of layoffs happening during that time, but I didn't think that it would affect me. Unfortunately, I had no savings to help hold me over between jobs.

The moment of truth hit me like a ton of bricks, and I had to face the reality that I would not be able to survive without a steady paycheck. I was living paycheck to paycheck, and although I was working hard and doing my best, it just wasn't enough. I was terrified because I knew that one day if anything bad was to happen, I would wind up homeless. Then, all the very things that I feared came upon me.

THE JOURNEY TO DESTINY

I convinced myself that I wasn't that concerned because I knew I could quickly pick up the pieces and get another job and not miss a beat. Well, that did not happen for me. It took months for me to find employment and months to receive an unemployment check. So, my last paycheck needed to stretch far because it would be a while before unemployment came into play. I had to be strategic with my spending of every penny and make some really hard decisions.

I decided to leave my apartment before I got evicted so that it would hopefully not affect my credit. The property management was kind enough to allow me to break my lease and pay the balance in installments. I rented a U-Haul truck and relocated my belongings to a storage facility. I had a few essentials in my car to dress if I was called for a job interview. I tried not to bring too much with me in case someone was kind enough to let me stay with them. After loading my car, I began calling my friends to see if I could sleep on their couches until I figured out what was I could do to get back on my feet. A few folks helped me out by offering their services for a day or two. Unfortunately, no one was ready to help me any further, so I hopped from pillar to pillar. I'm not sure which was more humiliating: the fact that I was homeless or that no one wanted to help me.

One day I received a promising lead from a friend who would allow me to stay with them. I just needed a little while at the person's house. My thoughts were that once I could get an unemployment check, I would be able to offer money to people and change people's willingness to help me. I stayed with a man that we will call Adam. Adam was and is a very nice person, and I was grateful for his willingness to help me. We had different lifestyles. While Adam was a person that liked to party, I was a private person that wanted quiet time to rest. Adam allowed me to sleep on his couch, but because he liked to have lots of wild parties in his house, I was constantly being shifted to accommodate his schedule. On the days he would have parties, I would have to leave, and sleep in my car. This started the saga of me just making up my mind to sleep in my car until I could figure things out.

While sleeping in my car, I reached out to more friends and family, but no one was willing to help. Since I did not look like I was struggling, I could not get anyone to believe that I had a hardship situation happening and I needed immediate help. I ended up homeless and living in my car for six months. I was in shock that this was happening to me. I managed to hold my head just barely above water until I started to drown.

Now that I had to accept that I had to live in my car, I had to figure out where I would park to be safe at night. I was advised to find 24-hour places that were well lit and stay there so I did. Large retail stores and fast-food restaurants were ideal locations. They were always full of people constantly going in and out, and it made me feel secure that if something were to happen to me, there would be witnesses to see it.

The Stranger

One evening while leaving my storage unit, I noticed a strange man was following behind my car. I thought I was imagining things until I moved to the right driving lane, and he moved to the right. I turned the street corner and he stayed on my trail and turned the corner also. That man was full blown stalking me. In my little white Chevy Cobalt, I floored it as fast as possible and took off down the 2-lane on Bankhead Highway in Atlanta. I was going 90 miles per hour in the dead of night looking to find someone that could help me and scare him off. Thankfully I was able to flag down a police officer at the gas station. I told him what was going on, and while I was talking with the officer, the stranger left. I stayed there long enough until I knew the guy was gone and wouldn't follow me anymore. I knew I wouldn't be safe sleeping in my usual spot, so that night, I found a hotel around the Six Flags area to camp out for the night. No matter how hard I tried to fall asleep, I couldn't. I was too afraid. I don't remember the last time I felt that afraid. I sat up looking around at the people coming in and out of the establishment, wishing that I had the money to get a room. I had to ration my cash to make my last check last because I had not received my unemployment check yet. I was in such a low place in my life and my spirit.

The next day, I found a church service nearby, it was just what I needed to receive some encouragement. I was going through so much; I needed a word from the Lord. I arrived at the church and when the service began, I felt rejuvenated. The praise and worship was amazing! I was anticipating the great word from the Lord that the pastor would deliver. The Lord knew what I was dealing with. That night, an Apostle spoke and gave prophetic words to the people in the audience, and before I knew it, he called me to stand up.

"You woman, watch your words. You have potent power when you speak, and the Lord will deal with you for unnecessary outcomes in people's lives due to your words."

Wait…What? Is this the word of God for me?

I was dumbfounded.

Surely the apostle must have been misinformed. I couldn't help but think about my situation and how so many people had rejected me. I thought to myself. I *am the victim here. People are mistreating me. And I'm the one that's homeless right now.*

I quickly had to shake that off because I was starting to become upset. Instead, I decided to receive the word in my heart, and I vowed to the Lord that I would do better. I gave in the offering that night from what little I had. There must have been something God was missing, but I wanted to be obedient. There is a song that says, when you cannot trust His hand, trust His heart. This was a moment when I needed to know that God had not forsaken me.

After the service that night, I returned to the Walmart parking lot and parked my car for the night. I wanted to fall asleep, but I couldn't shake what I had heard that night. *Could I have really been the problem?* I wondered. Thinking about what the pastor said to me caused me to analyze and consider whether I was using my words to destroy the lives of others. His words penetrated through me and caused me to take a deeper self-reflection. I had spent so much time blaming others but was there something more to this?

God what are you saying to me? I questioned.

Could I have been experiencing this trial because there was a part of me that spoke against others?

Of course, I knew what God's word said, "death and life are in the power of the tongue, and those who love it will eat its fruit," (Proverbs 18:2) but this was just too much for me to bear. Everyone was against me, yet I was the one called out and reprimanded by God.

But what about them?

Will they be able to get away with what they are doing to me? I questioned.

I felt at that moment that God had somehow skipped over the wrong they had done and had magnified my grumbling and complaining. It wasn't fair, and my natural mind could not comprehend why such a great burden had been placed on me. I didn't understand how this would lead me closer to my greatness.

CHAPTER 6

Sitting in My Hurt

A brother offended is more unyielding than a strong city, and quarreling is like the bars of a castle.
Proverbs 18:19

A true testament of our faith is when we can use the words that Jesus used on that cross, "Father forgive them for they know not what they do." It takes a lot of maturity to turn the other cheek and forgive others we feel don't deserve forgiveness. I had so much to reflect on after that night. I was getting accustomed to feeling sorry for myself, feeling like the victim, as I continued to deal with the pain of loss. I started to resent everyone around me and became angry. Self-pity took over, and I was constantly on the verge of losing it. I let bitterness take over my life by sitting in my hurt and refusing to let go of grudges; I didn't realize it because I thought I was surviving, but sadly I was doing myself more harm than good.

Living in the Reality

It was difficult to accept the reality that I was still sleeping in my car, even after receiving so many prophetic words about the great things that I would do for the Kingdom of God. I couldn't understand how my words in past times had created cars and apartments and other things I needed because of my faith and the power of my words, but nothing seemed to work this time. I had received words of knowledge about how I would be a great marketplace minister in business. Yet, in that state I did not look or feel like I could help anyone in the marketplace.

After so many negative occurrences, the seeds of bitterness started to take firm root in my life. But unfortunately, I didn't realize I was becoming bitter. The process started slowly, and before I knew it, it had become a stronghold. It began from unforgiveness and slowly graduated to resentment and bitterness. When bitterness rules one's life, it takes away all sense of normalcy. Being entrapped in bitterness is a vicious cycle that is hard to let go.

"All bitterness starts **out as hurt**. And your emotional pain may well relate to viewing whoever (or whatever) provoked this hurt as having malicious intent: As committing a grave injustice toward you; as gratuitously wronging you and causing you grief."[2]

Hebrews 12:15 (NIV) made the subject of bitterness clearer: "See to it that no one fails to obtain the grace of God; that 'no root of bitterness springs up and causes trouble, and by it many become defiled.'"

Bitterness defiles our soul and makes receiving from God and man hard. It's very subtle, and it seems justified in the way we react to the harm caused to us by others. It is a sin that catches us by surprise. It begins by peeking through the surface as a seedling of negative thoughts or complaining. It feeds off our emotions and any offense we have in our hearts."

2   Leon F. Seltzer, "Don't Let Your Anger "Mature" Into Bitterness," Psychology Today, January 14, 2015, https://www.psychologytoday.com/us/blog/evolution-the-self/201501/don-t-let-your-anger-mature-bitterness

The more I thought about those that turned their backs on me, the more bitter I became. It pained me to believe that people just wouldn't help me and left me to fend for myself. Everyone who knew me thought I was so strong and had life covered when that was the furthest thing from the truth! Maybe it was my tall stature that played a role in that. I am almost 6 feet tall, and I believe my physical appearance gave people the false impression that I was super resilient and could handle anything. I needed someone to say, yes, I'll help you as I had done for so many others. I needed help terribly, but I could not convince anyone to believe I had hit rock bottom.

Maybe if I showed people my bank account and that it was overdrawn, they would believe me, I thought. *Or if I removed my makeup off my face and looked very plain Jane, maybe that would have helped plead my case. Perhaps I should only wear clothes with holes in them.*

Based on the opinions of others, I simply did not look the part of a person that needed help. I couldn't prove to the world that I couldn't pull myself up without any help. People would periodically ask if I needed anything, and when I told them I did, they would say, "Oh, I don't have it." I caught on to what they were doing. They weren't inquiring out of compassion or sympathy. They were fishing for information about my struggle but were not genuinely interested in helping. This affected me and closed me off from telling my story of distress to anyone.

God Do You Hear Me?

Hear my prayer, O LORD; let my cry for help come to you. Do not hide your face from me when I am in distress. Turn your ear to me; when I call, answer me quickly. For my days vanish like smoke; my bones burn like glowing embers. Psalms 102:1

Have you ever felt as if God has turned his back on you? It's not uncommon for us to feel that way when on the journey to destiny. David cried out to God on many occasions when he felt distressed. I knew that feeling all too well. That period in my life was one of the darkest times for me. Depression and sadness overtook me as my whole world was turned upside down. I felt like God no longer heard my prayers. The onslaught from the forces of darkness was so strong, and I was sinking from the pain.

It seemed as if I was running for my life, yet I felt like Sarah when God said to Abraham that they would have a baby and she laughed. The prophecies I received were far away from the type of life I was living. On the contrary to this word, I was broke, busted, and completely disgusted. I was too broke to afford a roof over my head, and I was barely surviving eating peanut butter and jelly sandwiches morning, afternoon, and night. I knew better than to laugh at God, but I couldn't understand what was happening and how much longer I needed to suffer before I was completely saved from my troubles. It appeared as if everyone around me was flourishing, but it looked like God had utterly forgotten me. I felt alone but dared not complain. That is what got the children of Israel stuck and going in circles for 40 years and I didn't want to stay in my wilderness.

During that trial, I tried my best to remain positive. My spirit was willing to do everything God desired although my flesh was weak. During that time, I started listening to a lot of sermons in the car. During those isolated moments, the Holy Spirit would convict me about the bitterness and resentment I felt towards others. I knew I needed to forgive, but I simply didn't know how to do that. As I was honest and transparent with God about how I felt, I started to recognize the demonic strongholds that were holding me captive. I no longer recognized my thoughts.

I know the Bible says that deliverance is the children's bread, but I didn't have any bread. I needed to know where I could get deliverance from. My experience in the past with people led me to stay silent during that time to avoid judgment. I was already at a low place and didn't want to deal with the possibility of disappointment or hurt from letting someone know or inviting them into my life on a personal level. I felt justified to be upset about what I was experiencing, but if I sat any longer in my hurt and disgust, it would get worse than it already was. I was determined to face this demon of unforgiveness because that is exactly what it was.

Under Attack

It's a spiritual attack when you have tried to do everything you can and there's still a stronghold that you can't seem to shake. During that time, I was in a tailspin, constantly replaying the things that went wrong in my life. I questioned why I had to go through them, especially at such a young age. Upon reflection, I realized that what I was focusing on I was magnifying. The more

I talked about not being helped, the greater the bitterness and anger seemed to consume me. I knew I had to shift my focus on getting myself right with God and acknowledge that He was the only one that could save me.

As I cried out to God for help, I felt like I was being thrown into a pit like Joseph. Like Joseph, those close to me seemed to reject me the most. I keep wondering to myself, "Why?" Why did I have to be the one that goes through this? I didn't say it verbally, but it sure was in my heart for a very long time. At the time, I couldn't see past the pain and struggle. I imagined Joseph had a hard time seeing the purpose in his pain. But it was all a part of the preparation for what God was taking him to.

Harboring Resentment

"Resentment: a feeling of anger because you have been forced to accept *something that you do not like.*"[3] *Cambridge Dictionary*

What is resentment, and why do we hold on to it? These were the thoughts and questions I asked myself as I lay attempting to reconcile my hurt. It had festered within me, and I felt like a victim, but I couldn't let bitterness and resentment become a constant pitstop on my destiny. Of all the evil, destructive things that could happen to us, resentment is one of the worst. It is like a deadly germ. In resentment, recurring negative thoughts constantly work to gain power and control over us and destroy us.

---

3   "Resentment," Cambridge Dictionary, https://dictionary.cambridge.org/dictionary/english/resentment

No one in their right mind would harbor and nourish a deadly germ in his body, knowing that this germ would eventually kill him or her. Yet many Christians hold on to the sin of resentment, which is far more destructive than any germ. Resentment eats you up and holds you in a mental prison. This not only makes your soul exhausted but can make you physically sick.

After I acknowledged that I was holding resentment, I had to be honest about why I held on to these things for so long.

After prayer and reflection, I realized I held on to these things because:

- ✓ I felt justified.
- ✓ It made me feel superior.
- ✓ I was keeping score.
- ✓ I just enjoyed it.

Being Honest With Myself

It was time for me to face the resentment in my heart. I was constantly upset.

I needed to face the fact that I had a problem, and possibly if I had dealt with this in a better way years ago, I wouldn't have gotten to this point where the divorce, the church hurt, the homelessness and just trying to survive wouldn't have turned my life upside down. Hindsight is always 20/20. The best way for me to have handled this situation would have been to talk to a mentor or a life coach to help me navigate my way through my storms of life. I was overwhelmed and did not know the right way to go. I made such a mess with my life, that I no longer trusted myself to make good judgments or decisions concerning my life. At the time, I also did not have the resources to seek professional help.

I was good at brushing life situations under the rug; I always knew things would get better, "But when Lord?" is the question I frequently asked Him. I realized that faith did not replace the need to apply the life principles in my life. At some point, we must be honest and strip away the clutter and noise. We need to be honest with ourselves by reviewing our lives regularly and not avoiding our pain hoping that it will go away. It won't get better unless you decide it's time and are willing to put in the effort. You must acknowledge and not dismiss your pain and hurt.

Not Trusting Anyone

Not being able to trust anyone was part of my problem. I didn't trust that anyone truly cared or was concerned about what I was going through. But even after all of this, God was pulling me to release and trust Him. I knew He had a plan and I needed to do my part and let go of the grudges so that I could move on in my life. I'd done this my entire life because I didn't want to deal with my hurt and pain. I felt that if I acknowledged it, it was real; if I didn't, it wasn't real, which gave me false hope. I also expected God to fix it; I didn't feel obligated to deal with it because I believed God was the one who was supposed to fight my battle. I felt God was my vindicator, so I didn't have to be concerned. I overlooked the fact that God has already provided us with everything we require.

I had no idea that God had already taken care of this. All I needed to do was take action for healing to happen. He has provided the tools to each of us, but it is our responsibility to take care of what he has provided. God will not appear out of nowhere to solve our problems. He has outfitted you with everything you require. We must exercise caution when dealing with our pain, and decide not to wallow in it, and be willing to be honest with ourselves. To obtain freedom and deliverance from hurt and bitterness, you must be honest with yourself and be willing to put in the effort to be completely liberated.

I held onto my resentment way too long. It turned into bitterness and matured into a terminal illness that I had to fight. It was only at this point that I decided I would have to let it go so that I could finally be free. Sitting in your hurt is when you are constantly replaying the wrongs that others have said and things, they've done to you. I am sure many of us have been there before. When someone wrongs us, we replay the incident in our heads repeatedly, constantly wondering what we did to deserve the pain and hurt of others. When we think about those things repeatedly, we can become bitter and hateful because we've allowed the pain to fester too long. You're probably wondering if we shouldn't feel or express our emotions. It's okay to have emotions. Your emotions are valid, and God created them, but do you think God would want them to control you? No! And this is because the devil takes advantage of you when your emotions take control.

God doesn't want this for us. Ephesians 4:26 states, "Be angry but do not sin; do not let the sun go down on your anger, and do not make room for the devil." Anger is not sin in and of itself; our Lord Himself felt it (Mark 3:5) at the "hardness of men's hearts;" however, it is not to be brooded over and stimulated; beware of anger and ungoverned passions, and do not cherish anger. Do not sleep on it.

When you constantly repeat the hurt done to you in your mind, keeping a list of offenses, remembering details of things they said that hurt months or years ago, you will find it hard to have quiet moments. When I was in this phase of my life, I did my best not to have quiet moments. Having these moments meant that I needed an audio distraction everywhere I went. In the car, I kept the radio on. In the house, the television constantly played, and at night I had to have something playing so that I couldn't think about these things. The more you dwell and think about all the things that have gone wrong in your life, the deeper the ditch you dig. Like a natural ditch, the deeper it gets, the harder it becomes to get out on your own. The ditch is a reminder that we are all in need of God's mercy. He patiently waits with outstretched arms to pull us out of our ditch.

When others hurt us, we must forgive quickly and don't allow our emotions to overcome us. Letting things go and forgiving quickly is for you. Forgiving quickly helps you to hear without bias from God. It also improves your general well-being and health. Like Joseph, my process was preparation for the people to whom I have been called. God reminded me of scripture in Mark 10:18 "Are you able to drink from the cup that I drink, or be baptized with the baptism which I have been baptized with?" It was a reminder that for the Glory that needed to be revealed through me, there was a suffering that was required to qualify me for it. The children, the divorce, battle with low self-esteem, dealing with the church's hurt, and homelessness were all a part of my cup. I began to recite affirmations of who I was.

"You are strong, and You are courageous.

You are all God has called you to be and you've got this."

I said these affirmations until I started to believe their truth.

CHAPTER 7

The Cancer Scare

Therefore, having these promises, beloved, let us cleanse ourselves from all defilement of flesh and spirit, perfecting holiness in the fear of God.
2 Corinthians 7:1 (NASB)

I t was time for me to face my demons and deal with all the things I had been dwelling on. The hurts and the disappointments of my life started to take a toll on me spiritually, emotionally, and physically and I wanted to get my mind off all of that. *If I could just focus on doing something else like working on some projects, maybe that would take my mind off everything that was going on in my life*, I thought.

I needed to get busy to keep my mind from thinking about my hurt. In theory, I already knew how to cast down vain imaginations and everything that exalts itself against the knowledge of God (2 Corinthians 10:5), but it was easier said than done. Due to my personality type, I needed something that could distract me from what I was feeling. I was hiding from myself and my emotions. The truth is, I didn't want to face the reality that I was angry. I didn't want to admit that I had become upset with God even as a believer.

I attempted to keep my mind occupied to keep me from experiencing recurring cycles and negative thoughts. I thought maybe with my mind being occupied, it would help me get delivered and change my perspective, allowing me to move past it all. So, I decided to shift my attention and pour myself into giving and helping others through a non-profit I started in 2009 called Fresh Fire International Ministries Inc. It felt good to help others in need. It felt good to help parents provide the essentials for their children. Donating supplies, food and clothing while witnessing the relief on their parents' faces always made me feel good.

I recognized the look of desperation and feelings of hopelessness all too well, and I knew God had called me to be a blessing. Oftentimes I filled a void that I felt others didn't for me, but isn't that just how God works? He allows us to experience the trials in our lives so that we can offer compassion to others. I believe that is the true grace of a believer. Being able to love and serve because we know that our Heavenly Father will fill any areas of void and hurt in our lives. In the last chapter, I expressed how bitterness and hurt had to be released. During the time I was going through loneliness and depression I didn't realize what I needed to do to make the pain stop.

In 2020, I had a strong desire to do even more in my community. I was self-funding many of the contributions to keep the non-profit afloat and relying on donations from my local community to help. I came up with an idea to create funding for my organization to help reach more people in need. I noticed that we were receiving so many donated items, and I didn't have the capacity to hold them in one location, so I decided to open a thrift store. I had some previous experience working at Goodwill and knew what I needed to run the operation and get everything set up.

Opening the thrift store was not only a good idea for the community, but it was also good for me to keep my mind off the pain I was still battling through emotionally and mentally. Although I was beginning my healing process, it was still a tough time for me. The more I prayed, the more I wondered if God heard me. Despite how I was feeling, I still knew I had a mandate on my life to serve the brokenhearted.

When the project started, I immersed myself into opening the store. I rolled up my sleeves, found a store location, turned on the utilities, purchased the hardware materials and the shelving for the walls, and did whatever else was necessary to get the store open as soon as possible.

One day while working, I noticed the pain that I was feeling emotionally and mentally started manifesting in my physical body. In addition, I felt exhausted all the time, which was unlike me because I had always been a very hardworking and energetic person. As I put the store together, I became weaker. Finally, I went to the doctor and expressed that I didn't feel well.

The doctor asked, "What is causing you discomfort?"

"I don't know, but I just don't feel good. I'm tired all the time. I barely have any energy, and I need energy. I have been taking my multivitamins, Zinc, and Vitamin B, but I'm exhausted. Can you please check some blood work or do something?" I responded.

She set up a follow-up appointment to run some tests for my blood work, and she took an x-ray. When I received the results, I was surprised that everything returned fine. However, when she told me that everything was fine, I was mortified because I knew my body and something wasn't right. My energy was so low that I didn't even feel like getting out of bed in the morning. I was also barely eating because I had no appetite, yet I gained weight. I felt so bloated although I wasn't drinking a lot of water. *What is wrong with me?* I questioned.

Things worsened, and I started to feel like I was three months pregnant, then five months, and then I felt like I was ready to give birth. I didn't understand what was going on, but the entire time, throughout multiple tests and x-rays, the doctor kept insisting that everything was okay. Finally, one day at the doctor's office, I couldn't take it anymore. I needed answers. I banged my hand on the table in her office and told her to look again.

"There's something wrong… something's not right. There's something else, and we have got to find it!" I pleaded with her.

The doctor scheduled me for a CAT scan, and I waited three weeks for an appointment. While I waited, so many thoughts rushed through my mind about what could have been going on in my body. *Why am I feeling so badly?* I had been a person who had a few illnesses here and there throughout my life, but nothing major like that. At that point, this one didn't feel like it was something small because of all the physical changes I was experiencing. I dared not even look up the symptoms on WebMD because I didn't want to make myself even more afraid by stressing over the worst-case scenario. I didn't want my mind to play tricks on me and make it worse. I had been doing enough of that in my everyday life. I just decided to wait and hear what the doctor's office had to say.

The Results

"Sheila, we're going to have to schedule you to see an oncologist," my doctor told me.

These words were the last thing I thought I would ever hear. I had been waiting for three weeks to have the CAT scan, and after a brief few days of waiting for the results, I began to wonder if I would be okay. I had worked in the medical industry, and I was familiar with some medical terms. For sure, I knew what oncology meant.

I have cancer! I thought to myself

I was so perplexed.

"How soon can I get in there to see this doctor?" I responded.

"What we have to do is we have to schedule the appointment and they have to call you."

I waited for another three weeks before receiving a phone call to schedule the appointment. During the wait, I kept asking God, "why do I have to go through all this again after all the hardship I've gone through in my life?" It just didn't seem fair after the whirlwind I had previously experienced that I would be facing another life setback. I couldn't understand why life kept presenting these curveballs that knocked me flat on my back.

When the appointment date arrived, I went alone. I didn't want anyone to come with me because I wanted to process whatever news they were going to tell me before anyone else knew about it. There's a story in the Bible where Jesus was performing healing on Jarius' daughter, and before he could heal her, he put everyone out of the room (Matthew 5:37-43). At that moment, I related and felt it was best I hear the news myself. I felt I could hold it together if I were alone.

I don't know if you have ever received shocking news while you have been with anyone, but if you have, you know how emotional some people can be when they receive unexpected news. If you are not careful, their doubt will interrupt your faith and cause you to question whether you'll receive what you believe God for.

There were three doctors, including the main doctor, and schedulers responsible for the procedure during the appointment. They explained very carefully what they thought I was dealing with. They hadn't yet thoroughly reviewed all the CAT Scan films from my doctors, but they saw a picture of it and were able to give me a heads up. They were waiting to get the actual film to be able to make a diagnosis when I heard the words "stage three ovarian cancer" slip out.

I froze. I had to let that settle in for a moment...*stage three ovarian cancer?*

I looked straight ahead at her when the doctor said those words without blinking. I must have had a glazed look as I looked at her because she did her best to break my silence.

"New York Yankees. What part of the turnpike are you from?" she asked.

I was wearing a Yankees mask, and it was the first thing she could quickly grasp at to break the tension in the room. Whenever a person makes a statement like that, I know that person is from either New York or New Jersey.

I smiled, and I said, "Exit 11."

"Yeah. I figured that because people from Central and North Jersey tend to like the Yankees. People from 11 and lower on the turnpike tend to like the Phillies because they're closer to Philadelphia," she warmly responded.

That tiny, insignificant conversation made me feel so at ease. There was an immediate connection, and I felt like I had a fellow Jerseyan taking care of my medical needs. I cannot tell you how good I felt at that point when she made the comment because even with such a devastating diagnosis, God sent an angel to show me He was still there with me.

This was another difficult stop on my road to my destiny. I must admit, it didn't make sense to me at the time. Why do such bad things happen to good people? Although, I tried to fight back the negative thoughts and be in the moment, it was one of the hardest things I had ever done.

After we finished having the small talk about where we're from, I proceeded,

"I want to get this done as soon as possible. I want to be the next person that goes in for the surgery."

She obliged as she noticed the eagerness in my voice to get the procedure over with. The doctor scheduled the surgery for the following week. She explained her plans to take a biopsy with the hopes of removing most of the cancer. If that weren't successful, she would then treat the cancer with Chemotherapy. After my approval and agreement with the treatment plan, I signed the consent forms.

On the way home more thoughts replayed through my mind. I couldn't understand how cancer was sitting in my body. I wasn't an unhealthy person, and I took care of myself as best as I could. How could someone that had such a close relationship with God suffer this way? I needed answers.

During my quiet reflections, the Holy Spirit started to bring revelation about the hurt and bitterness that I harbored against others. It was as if it all began to flash before me. The spirit of revelation began to show me that the hurt I harbored was releasing toxins in my body.

Was it my hurt, bitterness, and anger that had caused this cancer? Could that have been the reason why I was physically sick? Would I have to bear the punishment for the pain that was inflicted on me? Why God? At that moment, I knew what I needed to do.

Holding onto a grudge can significantly impact your mental and physical health. "When we hold onto grudges and resentment, it's like drinking poison and expecting the other person to get sick," says Angela Buttimer, MS, NCC, RYT, LPC, a licensed psychotherapist at Thomas F. Chapman Family Cancer Wellness at Piedmont. "It causes us to carry negative, tense energy in our biology."[4]

I needed to truly forgive and release the hurt that went all the way back to my childhood. I had to forgive those that I felt had wronged me. I had to forgive the church and the pastor. I had to forgive my ex-husband. I had to forgive the father of my children. But most importantly, I had to forgive myself. Forgiving myself might have been the hardest out of all of the things I had to release.

Preparing for Surgery

The following Monday morning, I arrived at the hospital for my surgery in good spirits. I had been praying and fasting, and I had my prayer partners fasting and praying for me as well. There was a good prayer chain going for my positive outcome in the surgery and that everything would be okay.

The nurses at the OU Medical Center were amazing. They were absolutely reassuring and so positive. They gave me a warm blanket to keep me as I waited. My surgery was performed and afterwards they escorted me to the operating room. I saw my doctors and the anesthesiologist shortly before the procedure, and my OBGYN doctor, who would be doing the surgery. I felt much better after seeing her. They placed me under anesthetics, and I quickly drifted off. I awoke over eight hours later,

---

4   "What Does Holding a Grudge do to Your Health," Piedmont Healthcare, https://www.piedmont.org/living-better/what-does-holding-a-grudge-do-to-your-health, (accessed January 2022)

THE JOURNEY TO DESTINY

completely unaware of what had happened. This was meant to be a four-hour surgery, but it took twice as long because of complications. Four quarts of blood were lost because I couldn't maintain enough blood flowing to me, so they had to insert a needle into my jugular vein in my neck, but the good news was, she was able to remove 98 percent of the malignancy. To deal with the remaining 2%, I had to undergo Chemotherapy.

Now that the doctor had removed 98 percent of the cancer inside me, it was time for me to heal and get out of the hospital. While being in the hospital and getting rolled back into my room, was when I found out all that happened to me when I was in surgery. When I saw my doctor, we both looked exhausted, and she called me a fighter. I had lost so much blood that she struggled to keep me alive, but she fought hard for me as well. Not only did she fight, but the people in my corner that were praying for me were the real heroes! They held up the doctor's hands for eight hours while she was performing the surgery.

The doctor told me that I needed four pints of blood and may need more later. One of the other life altering things that happened to me while in surgery was; that I had to have a colostomy bag placed on my body. When I saw it, I almost screamed because I did not want to live with a "bag." The doctor assured me that it was temporary, but I still didn't like it. So, the thought of leaving the hospital with the "bag," a catheter, and everything else made me feel that there was an urgency to my letting the resentment and bitterness go and fast.

I thanked my doctor, and she said she would see me later and left. When the nurse came back into the room, I complained to her that I was having a hard time breathing. They looked at my oxygen levels and said it appeared almost perfect. I said, "trust me, I know my body." They did a CAT scan and found that I had two blood clots in my lungs. Once I found that out, I became nervous because I knew that situation was very dangerous. They said they would take me downstairs to do another type of surgery and break up the clots by blasting them out. I did not like how that sounded, and I started to pray silently.

As I was being wheeled down to yet another procedure, I quietly heard the voice of the Lord say, "They will not find those clots. I just removed them." I smiled and told the person wheeling me to the procedure that they would not find the clots. He looked at me as if I was still delirious from the surgery, but I smiled and turned back around. They gave me anesthesia and put me under. After the anesthesia wore off, the first thing the doctor said to me was "I couldn't find the clot." It was just like the Lord said it would happen. They rolled me back to my hospital room and they decided to look for more clots. They found one and a big one in my left leg. They then put me on blood thinners to take care of that one.

As I was laying in the room, I meditated on how I got here. Did my bitterness, hurt and anger land me in the hospital bed? A resounding 'yes' was my answer. Unfortunately, holding on to (my) resentment forced me onto my sickbed. I stayed in the hospital for a week and was ready to go home. I told myself I had to mentally prepare for the chemo. Before I could deal with the Chemotherapy, I had to deal with the root cause of my diagnosis: anger, unforgiveness, and bitterness, and the rest of the emotions that were related to it.

After experiencing the surgery and the mental and emotional toll it took on my body, I concluded that holding on to anything toxic is not worth it. Had I not been hit with this affliction; I would probably be still sitting in my hurt. Going through that trial had made me ask myself, *was it worth holding on to the hurtful things that people did?* I even questioned their motives. *Did some of them intentionally mean to hurt me? Did I blow some of it out of proportion? Did I really have to go through this in the first place? If I had simply forgiven, could I have escaped having to be scared and deal with chemo?* In my heart I knew that the answer was a resounding 'yes.' I didn't want to go through Chemotherapy with unforgiveness in my heart and risk the chance of cancer again. It wasn't worth it. But even more than not wanting the cancer to reoccur, I wanted to please God with my life. I wanted to receive God's forgiveness. Matthew 6:14 states, "For if you forgive other people when they sin against you, your heavenly Father will also forgive you."

CHAPTER 8

Forgiveness is a Choice

" For if you forgive other people when they sin against you, your heavenly Father will also forgive you. But if you do not forgive others their sins, your Father will not forgive your sins."

Matthew 6:14-15

Psychologists define forgiveness as a conscious, deliberate decision to release feelings of resentment or vengeance toward a person or group who has harmed you, regardless of whether they deserve your forgiveness.[5] God requires that we forgive others if we want to enter the Kingdom of Heaven. Once I acknowledged the hurt of my past, I had to accept that forgiveness was a choice that I needed to make.

Understanding what forgiveness is not, is just as important as defining what forgiveness is. Experts who study or teach forgiveness make it clear that when you forgive, you do not minimize or deny the gravity of an offense committed against you. Forgiveness provides the forgiver with peace of mind and liberates him or her from corrosive anger, which can lead to bitterness. [4] Although I was clueless about how to forgive, I knew that it was actually for my own good.

---

5   "What is Forgiveness?" Greater Good Magazine, https://greatergood.berkeley.edu/topic/forgiveness/definition , (accessed December 2021)

Why Forgive?

Forgiveness liberates your soul, and it allows you to receive the blessings of God. Think of it like this, if you want to receive something from someone, but your hands are closed and turned downwards, how can you receive it? You can't, right? The same concept applies to forgiveness. You will never be able to receive what God has for you if you are not willing to release what you are holding on to.

God is very compassionate and forgiving that He constantly demonstrates forgiveness in the Bible. God forgave man even before we even realized we offended God. Unforgiveness stems from hurt and as commanded by the word of God, it's mandatory to forgive so God can also forgive your sins.

"And forgive us our trespasses, as we forgive them that trespass against us."

Matthew 6:12

When the Holy Spirit began to convict me about forgiveness, I pondered on what would at least happen if I tried to forgive. What could it hurt if I tried to walk in forgiveness? As bad as my life was, I was willing to try anything. It was my last-ditch effort before I completely walked away from God and life as I know it.

In the book of Matthew forgiveness is addressed, "Then Peter came to Jesus and said, "Lord, how many times shall I forgive my brother or sister who sins against me? Up to seven times?" Jesus answered and said, "I tell you, not seven times, but seventy-seven times."

After reading that passage again, I felt a nudge in my spirit to work on that area in my life, but I needed answers on how to do it. God gave me an idea and impressed on my heart to embark on a fast to be able to start the forgiveness process. I finally made the decision that I would forgive, and I would never go back to that place of darkness and depression. So, I proclaimed a fast and asked the Lord to help me change my heart and soul on the matter of unforgiveness. I knew that He would do it because I needed his help, and I didn't have the strength within myself to do it.

Joel 2:42 says, "Call on me on the day of trouble. I am the one who delivers, rescues, and redeems. And I will do it." I held on to His promise that He would help me. I held on to this word.

After meditating on the word and releasing the pain from the people, I began to feel a freedom that I had never experienced before. I would always be willing to rehearse the hurts to anyone that asked me how I was doing. That changed and I noticed that I stopped doing that. Now, when I am asked how I am doing, I say, "great." Some days I will say it by faith, and other days it is great. I will not say this was an immediate deliverance. It required a lot of hard work and determination, however, I believed in the Lord and His Word, and I did my part to experience its wholeness.

The next major transformation I experienced was in my thoughts. One day I started noticing that the focus of my thoughts shifted. Before then, I used to magnify the hurt daily. After a time, I would think about it maybe a day a week and before long, I was no longer meditating on it at all. Now I was ready for my chemotherapy treatments. Going through Chemotherapy is a challenging ordeal. You are dealing with the effects that chemo physically does to your body. You constantly want to throw up. You are weak and always feeling fatigued. When you add a major surgery to having chemo, I felt that I just wanted to die. I had to push through it, take it one day at a time, and walk through the process. I had six rounds of chemo every three weeks. To be ready to take the chemo, your body had to be prepared to accept it. Your blood levels must be above a certain amount, or they will not allow you to take it. I thought about that in the spirit. I had to spiritually be ready to accept God's forgiveness for myself and what I did in my life.

What I was doing by holding on to the bitterness and unforgiveness was a flat-out sin. Yes, I was willingly holding on to a SIN and feeling completely justified, but this is what the Lord says about my sin. I referenced this scripture earlier, but this version has a different interpretation. "Looking carefully lest anyone falls short of the grace of God; lest any root of bitterness springing up cause trouble, and by this becomes defiled" Hebrews 12:15 (NKJV).

I was a Christian that loved the Lord, and I knew that scripture, but something different happened when I read it this time. I desire to be pleasing in the Lord's sight. How can I please Him when I am defiled? I cannot. I repented to the Lord, and I wanted to do better in His sight.

Pleasing the Lord requires grace and faith. You'll struggle if you want to please God with your own strength. The Bible also tells us that without Faith, it is impossible to please God. It is by faith you receive salvation, and after salvation, you need the grace of God to help you live the path that continually pleases Him.

For it is by grace you have been saved, through faith and this is not from yourselves, it is the gift of God not by works, so that no one can boast. For we are God's handiwork, created in Christ Jesus to do good works, which God prepared in advance for us to do".

Ephesians 2:8-9

For before he was taken, he was commended as one who pleased God. And without faith it is impossible to please God, because anyone who comes to him must believe that he exists and that he rewards those who earnestly seek him.

Hebrews 11:5-6, NIV

A few months later, something marvelous happened to me. Someone asked me about a situation that I was wronged in, and my first reaction was not to tell how badly the person mistreated me like I once did. My reaction was to cover them and not talk about them. Instead, I silently prayed for them. *Whoa! What a change.* I startled myself with that response. It became apparent that God was changing me and my heart. I was relieved to know that I was being delivered so that I could do and be all that the Lord had called me to be.

We live in a fallen world, which means we will face hurt and offense every day. Very often, it is the people that are closest to us that will hurt us the most. If you think about it, random people cannot hurt you because you are not in a relationship with them. Bitterness and/ or unforgiveness are the front door gates that the enemy gains access to attack us. Unforgiveness and bitterness are invisible chains that imprison us and hinder our relationship with God. When we choose not to forgive, it is without a doubt a primary way that gives the enemy the right to attack Christians. The words, actions, and inactions of others (and ourselves) can wound us to the core. Things like neglect and abuse, violence, betrayal, cruel words and more can cause bitterness and resentment to take root in our hearts. If not dealt with we will find ourselves in situations that open the doors for attack on our lives.

As believers we must forgive even when we feel the offender is not deserving of it. Forgiveness is not a feeling; it is a decision and a choice of your will or mind. We can uproot it if we choose to. I can hear someone asking, "What does that mean?" It may be difficult to forget, but forgiving is not the same as forgetting. Forgiveness is a choice and here is what the scripture says: "Be angry and yet do not sin; do not let the sun go down on your anger, and do not give the devil an opportunity." Ephesians 4:26-27.

At the end of the Lord's prayer, Jesus warns us, "For if you forgive others for their transgressions, your heavenly Father will also forgive you. If you do not forgive others, then your Father will not forgive your transgressions." Matthew 6:14-15

He who hates his brother or sister is in darkness and walks in darkness and does not know where he or she is going, because the darkness has blinded his eyes. 1 John 2:11

Why is forgiveness so important to the Lord? One simple answer is that He wants us to experience freedom, not the chains of anxiety and roots of bitterness that bind us when we don't forgive. God loved the world so much that He had to send His Son for the atonement of our sins. Christ wants us to model His lifestyle. Even when we were undeserving of this forgiveness, yet He forgives us. Forgiveness is for us, not for the person who offended us or did us wrong. His heart is for us to fully experience the authentic life that He created for us. If our hearts are filled with anger or bitterness, there will be no room for the Holy Spirit to dwell and fellowship with you. The Holy Spirit is a spirit of truth and can't dwell where it's defiled.

Unforgiveness Creates a Gap Between You and God

You may be wondering how you can genuinely forgive from the heart? First, you must acknowledge the hurt or hate you have towards the person. Don't try to limit or suppress the pain. Be honest with your feelings, and if your forgiveness doesn't visit the emotional core of the offense, it will be incomplete. Let God bring it to the surface so that He can deal with it. This is where the healing takes place. Now it is time to be set free and break these chains.

Without you truly turning things over to the Lord, He will not handle it for you. Why should He? By holding on it you are saying that you have it, and you don't need help. Because you are still dealing with whatever emotion you're feeling, i.e., anger, bitterness, etc. This is not to say that you won't feel something when you are offended because you will. What has worked for me is, I literally quote the scripture in my mind and remind myself that the Lord will take care of whatever the situation. You need to believe that Justice, recompense, and payback is your portion. Though forgiveness can help repair a damaged relationship, there is no obligation to reconcile with the person who harmed you or release them from What they did wrong to you.

Instead, forgiveness brings the forgiver peace of mind and frees him or her from their own anger. At the same time, there is some debate over whether true forgiveness requires positive feelings towards the offender. I would say that it does not. It mainly involves letting go of deeply held negative feelings. Doing that empowers you to recognize the pain you suffered without letting that pain define you, enabling you to heal and move on with your life.

Why Should We Practice Forgiveness?

We often think of forgiveness as a kind of mercy or compassion extended to someone who wronged us. While that can be true, I have found that in my own life over the past few years has revealed some enormous personal benefits to forgiveness as well. Forgiveness makes us happier: I have found that when I have forgiven people, I can move on and I am much happier because I took care of the offense. You must understand that forgiveness is a process. True forgiveness doesn't happen instantly; instead, it takes time and energy to achieve and might not come easily, with persistence it will happen.

I would like to offer 20 Bible verses that will help with the process of forgiveness. It will be challenging, but it is not impossible. If I was able to forgive, you can too! If you meditate on the scriptures and put them into action, you will see the change in your life.

1. Matthew 6:14 - "For if you forgive other people when they sin against you, your heavenly Father will also forgive you."

2. Colossians 3:13 - "Bear with each other and forgive one another if any of you has a grievance against someone. Forgive as the Lord forgave you."

3. Ephesians 4:32 - "Be kind and compassionate to one another, forgiving each other, just as in Christ God forgave you."

4. Luke 6:37 - "Do not judge, and you will not be judged. Do not condemn, and you will not be condemned. Forgive, and you will be forgiven.

5. Matthew 18:21-22 - "Then Peter came to Jesus and asked, "Lord, how many times shall I forgive my brother or sister who sins against me? Up to seven times?" Jesus answered, "I tell you, not seven times, but seventy-seven times."

7. Mark 11:25 - "And when you stand praying, if you hold anything against anyone, forgive them, so that your Father in heaven may forgive your sins."

8. Psalm 86:5 - "You, Lord, are forgiving and good, abounding in love to all who call to you."

9. Psalm 32:1 - "Blessed is the one whose transgressions are forgiven, whose sins are covered."

10. 1 John 1:9 - "If we confess our sins, he is faithful and just to forgive us from our sins and cleanse us from all unrighteousness."

11. Matthew 6:15 - "But if you do not forgive others for their sins, your father will not forgive your sins."

12. Hebrews 8:12 - "For I will forgive their wickedness and will remember their sins no more."

13. Proverbs 17:9 - "Love prospers when a fault is forgiven but dwelling on it separates close friends."

14. Proverbs 10:12 - "Hatred stirs old quarrels, but love overlooks insults."

15. Psalm 103:12 - "As far as the east is from the west, so far has he removed our transgressions from us."

16. Isaiah 43:25 - "I, even I am he who blots out your transgressions for my own sake and remembers your sin no more."

17. Daniel 9:9 - "The Lord our God is merciful and forgiving, even though we have rebelled against him."

18. Hebrews 10:17 - "Then he adds: "Their sins and lawless acts I will remember no more."

19. Ephesians 1:7-8 - "In Him we have redemption through His blood, the forgiveness of sins, according to the riches of His grace which He made to abound towards us in all wisdom and prudence."

20. Psalm 130:3-4 - "If you, Lord should mark iniquities, O Lord who could stand? But there is forgiveness with You, that You may be feared."

CHAPTER 9

Destined to Win

Fight the good fight of the faith. Take hold of the
eternal life to which you were called and about
which you made the good confession
in the presence of many witnesses.
1 Timothy 6:12 (NIV)

t's good to serve a God that wants us to win. He is always looking out for our best interest in everything we do. In fact, God desires nothing more than for us to win and overcome the world's trials. 2 Corinthians 2:14 states, "Now thanks be unto God, which always causeth us to triumph in Christ, and maketh manifest the Savior of His knowledge by us in every place."

No matter the challenges and circumstances, He wants to see that we triumph. God created us to win in every facet of our life; spiritually, physically, financially, and naturally. He detests mediocrity as a child of God. Therefore, He continually admonishes us and constantly guides us through His Word. Unfortunately, many Christians think it's unbiblical and wrong to focus on winning. They would rather focus on the struggle than the victory that awaits them if they persevere in their trials. Perhaps if they understood that winning isn't a prideful act, they would create an atmosphere for victory over their circumstances.

Let me also add that winning isn't about you proving the naysayers wrong. God isn't interested in you winning over people but rather over your circumstances and tribulations. The Bible tells us that, "we wrestle not against flesh and blood, but against principalities, against powers, against the rulers of the darkness of this world, against spiritual wickedness in high places.: (Ephesians 6:12).

Winning is Our Birthright

God created us in His image and gave us dominion over all things, so I believe winning is our birthright. By not exercising the power we have been given, we will live our lives short on the promises of God for us. If only we could trust Him and put our hope in Him, we'll win on every side.

Our Heavenly Father is a winner, and since man was created in God's image and likeness, then redeemed man must be designed to be a winner. In fact, after God made Adam and Eve, He commanded them to go win! Look at the verse in Genesis 1:28,

"And God blessed them. And God said to them, "Be fruitful and multiply and fill the earth and subdue it and have dominion over the fish of the sea and over the birds of the heavens and over every living thing that moves on the earth."

And lets also reflect and meditate on Romans 5:5,

"And hope does not put us to shame, because God's love has been poured out into our hearts through the Holy Spirit, who has been given to us"

After feeling that I was the cause of what was going on in my body, I knew that it was time to make a permanent change. This is not to say that every illness that comes upon a person is solely related to the hurt and bitterness in their lives but in my opinion, it plays a big part. For me to be free and stay free, I had to come up with a mechanism for handling hurt.

Beloved, never avenge yourselves, but leave it to the wrath of God, for it is written "Vengeance is mine, I will repay, says the Lord" Romans 12:19-21 (ESV). To the contrary, "if your enemy is hungry, feed him; if he is thirsty, give him something to drink; for by doing, you will heap burning coals on his head. Do not be overcome by evil but overcome evil with good."

What exactly does the "heap burning coals' 'mean? Proverbs 25:22 Explains that very nicely. It means to cause someone to feel remorse by repaying good for evil. I have heard this my entire life. However, I never put this scripture to use because I felt justified in my pain and hurt, and no one could tell me that I did not have a right to take matters into my own hands. Look where that got me. I would not wish cancer on my worst enemy. But, with my new mindset of living, it is in the Lord's hands. I know that He will take care of whatever injustice that I face.

The Lord has my back, and He is the one keeping score, and I don't have to. The scripture says in Numbers 23:19 (NIV) that God is not a human, that He should lie, not a human being, and change his mind. Does He speak and then not act? Does He promise and not fulfill? Whatever you need help with you find that promise in His Word, the Lord has you! His Word is true and you can take His promise to the bank. Don't get discouraged in your journey. It's easy to feel discouraged, especially when you're faced with many tribulations, but God wants us to be of good cheer rather than being discouraged.

A Winner's Mindset

God's concept of winning is good news for everyone! Romans 8:37 states, "We are more than conquerors through Him that loved us." At this point, a religious mindset often takes over and says, "Yes, I'll be a winner someday because my reward is in Heaven." Of course, we have an eternal reward waiting for us in Heaven. But God's provision of victory applies now, to every human existence. We've been granted dominion here in this life, because we are "in Christ Jesus" and He said, "All power is given unto me in heaven and earth." (Matthew 28:18)

The power we have in Jesus makes us winners in this life! And the reward of the godly is victory in every area of life, health, prosperity and much more. It's one thing to know that God wants you to be a winner, but it's quite another thing to know how to become one. Philippians is a book about winning written by a winner, the apostle Paul. Though Paul experienced many difficulties in his life, he never lived under his circumstances. Instead, he lived above them and controlled them.

What is it that made Paul such an outstanding winner? How did he learn to walk the winner's way? Look at Philippians 3:12-14,

"Not as though I had already attained, either were already perfect: but I follow after, if that I may apprehend that for which also, I am apprehended of Christ Jesus. Brethren, I count not myself to have apprehended: but this one thing I do, forgetting those things which are behind, and reaching forth unto those things which are before, I press toward the mark for the prize of the high calling of God in Christ Jesus."

Look at the phrase, "...that I may apprehend that for which also I am apprehended of Christ Jesus." Paul knew God had apprehended him for a special purpose. So likewise, you too have a unique, divinely appointed destiny. If you want to be a winner, you must determine in your heart to pursue that divinely ordained destiny.

Paul also said, "...I count myself not to have apprehended." In other words, I haven't arrived yet. We should have this same mindset. You haven't arrived yet when it comes to enjoying everything God wants you to have. So don't ever get satisfied with the status quo.

Finally, Paul goes on to say, "I press toward the mark for the high calling of God in Christ Jesus." This is a crucial phrase. It contains four terms that represent the keys to finding and fulfilling God's destiny for your life as a winner. "Press," "mark," "prize," and "high calling."

Trying to Figure it Out Myself

I was not used to receiving help and figuring it out on my own became my normal. However, constantly complaining about not having help, created a dark cloud over me. I knew the scriptures of God saying, He was a present help in time of need, and He would not leave or forsake me, but I wanted a human presence to help me. I always thought if He was going to send help, He'd send someone to guide me. I didn't think He was the one that would give me instructions on how to do it. God was always there to point me in the right direction, but my lack of alignment with the plan of God for my life kept me in the wilderness longer than I needed to. I learned over time that the plans of God are wise and will always succeed. He wants us to lean on Him and bring all our burdens and cast our cares on Him. He's willing to teach us and guide us only if we allow Him.

Our Heavenly Father is concerned with the deep things in our hearts. Our attention to a personal relationship with Him dictates the time it takes to hear His heart concerning the matters of our hearts. God hears, but we must be willing to listen to His instructions. We shouldn't sit back and expect things to manifest without doing our part. This is not about helping God grant your heart's desires rather, it's more about listening and being ready to know what is required of us. Sometimes, He may require faith, sometimes actions. In my situation, He required me to be open to His way of handling things on my behalf. I had to release the misconceptions I had and take my mind off what others were willing to do for me. He required me to be okay with being alone until I had become the person He intended.

Reflections

You have read my testimonies about many situations the bitter root of unforgiveness has caused firsthand in my life, and these were but a few. While some may be able to sympathize with my encounters in this book, the intent was not to gather pity but rather to provide hope for those who find themselves in the cycle I had experienced.

It's to help show the power of a mindset shift and how to look for the good in every situation even though it may appear dismal. Let us give grace and mercy to others as we have so freely received in our shortcomings and choose to see the light in others even if it may be candle flame at the time. Let us heal so we don't project our brokenness on others and create a false assessment of those we encounter along our path. Believe that people are not always out to get us and hurt us.

I want this book to encourage you that no matter what circumstances you face, you can always triumph if you totally put your trust in God and never give up on your journey to being a better version of yourself.

The Mayo Clinic tells us the benefits of letting go of unforgiveness. They say that "Letting go of grudges and bitterness can make way for improved health and peace of mind. Forgiveness can lead to:

- Healthier relationships
- Improved mental health
- Less anxiety, stress and hostility
- Lower Blood pressure
- Fewer symptoms of depression
- A stronger immune system
- Improved heart health
- Improved self-esteem

The Mayo Clinic also suggested ways to reach a state of forgiveness. They stated, "Forgiveness is a commitment to a personalized process of change."[6] I believe the cross was the price for our freedom. As we too are partakers in Christ, we will experience suffering associated with the destiny God has for us. Though the price will be expensive, the reward for paying the price will be equally commensurate. The scripture says that "There is nothing too hard for God." Jeremiah 32:17. He will give you the desires of your heart, great and small, but you must believe that He can do it. You are not in this alone. He has you and will gladly help you.

The forgiveness piece is the beginning of your new life. Once you master this obstacle, new doors will open for you to walk into your destiny. Could it be the enemy wants you to stay stuck in this rut so that you don't see all that God has for you to do? This is a trick and a trap that has cost me years of my life. I can even go as far as saying decades of time that I allowed the enemy to steal from me. You don't have to let him to do the same to you. If you were like me, and the enemy has stolen years from you too, the good news is that there is recompense for those lost years. The Bible says, "But if he (the thief) be found, he must restore sevenfold; He may have to give up all the substance of his house. Proverbs 6:31 KJV.

The devil has been caught. We found him out! He was trying to make it hard for you to let this go but he can't keep you there. He must repay you for all your time wasted time. I have one more promise just for you. The Bible also says,

6   Mayo Clinic Staff, "Forgiveness: Letting go of Grudges and Bitterness," Mayo Clinic, Novemeber 13, 2020, https://www.mayoclinic.org/healthy-lifestyle/adult-health/in-depth/forgiveness/art-20047692#:~:text=Letting%20go%20of%20grudges%20and%20bitterness%20can%20make%20way%20for,Healthier%20relationships

"And I will restore to you the years that the locust hath eaten, the cankerworm, and the caterpillar and the palmerworm, my great army which I sent among you."

Joel 2:25 KJV

God Gives Beauty for Ashes

A winner's mindset will require us to release the weights of our past and look toward Jesus Christ, the author and the finisher of our faith. He is why we have the strength to run our race and become victorious in everything that we do. Looking back at every situation and hardship I've faced, I can't help but thank God for turning my mess into a message. I've realized that God's plans will always stand, and His will always will be done. Although I'm still a work in progress, God has changed my life beyond my imagination and given me a reason to be grateful for all I've experienced.

CHAPTER 10

God Will Restore

"Though you have made me see troubles, many and bitter, you will restore my life again; from the depths of the earth you will again bring me up. You will increase my honor and comfort me once again."

Psalms 71: 20-21

I'm Free!

Today I choose to live and be set free. This is now my new mindset. By God's grace, I have allowed my mind to set those people free. Your mind is the greatest battleground. God wants to use it to fulfill your destiny while the devil desires to destroy you with it.

> Jesus said, "Most assuredly, I say to you, whoever commits sin is a slave of sin. And a slave does not abide in the house forever, but a son abides forever. Therefore if the Son makes you free, you shall be free indeed."
>
> **John 8:34-36 NKJV**

As I reflect on the journey to destiny, I know better than to carry the pain and hurt from offense. I don't allow toxic ways to seep into my life. I no longer allow the negativity to consume me. I now know those that God truly calls will experience the biggest blows in life. Our faith will be tested more times than we can count, but it won't take us out. Although it was meant to destroy me, I believed the blow of cancer would not have the victory over my life. Instead, my story would end in victory.

I have helped counsel many people living in regret and carrying the weight of failed expectations. It's natural for us to want to see the best in life. But what isn't natural is when we tie our emotional and mental stability to the success or outcome of our life. We shouldn't internalize the hurt but instead we should seek getting the proper help to receive the emotional breakthrough we need. Although there are things we can control in life, there are some things that we can't.

Sadly, many of us stay sitting right there. We have experienced so much hurt that we don't know who to trust. Believe me I understand, but even when others mishandle us, God requires us to rise higher. Michelle Obama made a statement, "when they go low, we go high."[7] To our flesh this statement doesn't make sense. In fact, when they go low, we want to help them go lower. But as believers, we must align our lives with the Word of God and submit to His ways. He will never allow you to suffer more than you can bear.

I pray my story has helped you see how God uses all things to work together for our good on your journey of life. It's all a part of becoming who we have been destined to be. As I was writing this book, reflecting on how hard it was for me during that time, I began to think about the people that are struggling right now in

---

7   Raisa Bruner, "Michelle Obama Explains What Going High Really Means," Time, November 20, 2018, https://time.com/5459984/michelle-obama-go-high/

their lives during this pandemic. Losing a job and not knowing where your next paycheck will come from is not easy.

Many people can relate to my story due to the homelessness and hopelessness that the pandemic brought. In addition, many people are struggling financially and going through the hardest times of their lives. As I submitted to the process, I began to see the joy in my journey. After many people thought I would have quit, I connected to the hope we have in Christ, and I believed and expected a brighter outcome. I have always believed that if we stay connected to our Father, we would one day understand the "why" in what we consider setbacks and disappointments. The truth is these are the life lessons that shape us into greatness.

God is aware of all the things that happened in the past. All the circumstances we encountered shaped us into what He wants us to be. I am reminded of a famous saying "what doesn't kill you makes you stronger" and I understand that much better now. I realized that I went through everything to become the person I am today and bring liberation to others. My all-time favorite Bible verse also explains this.

"Count it all joy, my brothers, when you meet trials of
various kinds, for you know that the testing of your
faith produces steadfastness."

James 1:2

This Bible text brings hope to me. God makes us go through
trials to make us into who we are. Moreover, how do you grow
without overcoming challenges? We must be opened to seeing
and understanding the lessons when we go through different
phases. You only learn and grow if you're open to always seeing
the good in every challenge.

I have realized that the intensity of the ups and downs we
experience are often directly related to the call of our lives. For
those called to the Prophetic Office, depression is a major fight
we have to battle. Major highs then major lows, I believe the call
dictates the level of warfare that I have experienced.

I have received so many prophetic words that God is using my
voice to help bring hope and healing to others. I didn't understand
how He would do that. The enemy's job was to get me off focus
so I wouldn't see the outcome of the vision. That's what he does
to each of us that God has chosen. He sends all sorts of fiery
darts so that we will abort the call. I have had multiple words
about opening businesses for myself come to pass. The Ministry
of Helps I now lead was prophesied years before it happened.
Bringing hope to those in need gives me a great sense of purpose
in life.

Answering the Call

The Bible tells us in Matthew 22:14 "Many are called but few are chosen." God has many assignments to be fulfilled on the earth. God knew that there would be solutions needed for mankind and handpicked you to carry out a specific assignment. Sometimes, when we look at what we have been through and what our lives look like, we often question the call. The message to Joshua was to be strong and be of good courage, and just like Joshua, God is extending those words to you.

Say this out loud.

I, (Insert Your Name) am strong and of good courage.

(Say it as many times as you need to get it in your spirit.)

Before the earth's foundations, He knew you and ordained you for such a time as this. There is no better place to be than in the will of God for your life. When you are in God's will, He gives you peace even during storms. His will carries His protection and provision. When you are outside of His will, you feel unsure and unstable.

He Restored My Love Life

As God began to restore me, He also restored my love life. I wasn't actively pursuing a relationship, but I wasn't closed to the idea of getting married again one day. While living in Atlanta for 15 years I dated a bit, however, I became discouraged with the dating scene.

I had completely given up on love for years. Yet, I kept receiving so many prophetic words about love that was around the corner. I constantly rejected that idea internally. I did not trust my judgment in men because I always seemed to pick the wrong type of man. Choosing was not my strong point to say the least. The most pivotal word that I received was that I would meet a mature man that would love God and not take from me but add to my life and display the fruits of the spirit. I had no idea where he would appear from.

One day I received an amazing opportunity for a job promotion, and I decided to take it. That promotion also required a relocation from Georgia to Oklahoma. Before I arrived in Oklahoma, I decided to test the dating waters a bit. I was in a new environment. It was a different city and I believed it was a season of new opportunities and relationships. I was open to whatever God had planned for me. If this was my season of newness, I was not going to stand in the way and limit my blessings.

As a self-proclaimed house mouse, I knew it would be difficult as I spent most of my time at home. A Prophet told me, "He cannot find you while you are sitting in your house." He was right, but with my new job I constantly worked, so I knew that I would not find the type of man I was interested in in the circles that I frequented. I had heard online was a great place to meet people, so I gave it a try. I registered online for an account at Match.com and opened myself to the word of internet dating. My experience was good, I had several great dates, but there was one that stood out from the rest. Not too long after receiving that word, the position to Oklahoma immediately became available and I met a wonderful man. God has confirmed through my dreams on multiple occasions that he was the one for me. He was everything I needed and more. We married on March 1st, 2022.

The Journey to Your Destination- Winning at Life

No matter how bad life was, I am grateful for the wins I've achieved through the help of Christ. I won the cancer battle. I started a ministry that feeds and clothes the underserved population in my community. I launched an insurance company that sells Life, Health and Medicare and became a Notary. I will have an extension to the business teaching classes for financial literacy in the near future. I am living the life that was pre-destined for me.

More doors have continued to open, and in 2021 the State of Oklahoma asked me to be a part of their organization, "Be A Neighbor Oklahoma." The goal was to collaborate with my organization to provide clothing to people in need in the local area. Mayor Frank Calvin from the city of Spencer wrote my grant to help my 501c3 get funding. This was nothing but the grace and favor of God to provide such an amazing opportunity to help me secure the funding I needed to serve more families. The very thing that the enemy tried to destroy me with and kill my hope, years later God is using it for His Glory and funding the assignment. God is a restorer! My journey has been nothing short of miraculous.

As we come to the close of this journey together, I want you to be encouraged. Allow my life testimony to be a motivation for you. I want my stories to bring hope to those who have experienced a failed marriage. Or those that have battles with their health. Or anyone that has struggled financially. No matter what you are experiencing, that will not be the end of your story. Don't be embarrassed or ashamed about your journey. Always remember that you are more than enough. Any failures in life does not make you a failure. Because your marriage failed doesn't mean that you are a failure. Maybe the timing was off, maybe you rushed into it, maybe you ignored the red flags. Don't beat yourself up about whatever has happened in your life.

God doesn't make mistakes. We all have a God given purpose. We are not so far gone that God changes His mind about us. There is something in your life that you do well, and that could be the very thing that the Lord purposed and called you to do. Your life is important to God. As I have shared these wins with you, I hope that you will be encouraged to stay on course until you reach your destiny.

Therefore, my beloved brothers, be steadfast, immovable, always abounding in the Lord's work, because you know that your labor is not in vain in the Lord.

1 Corinthians 15:18

Bonus

30 Day Journey to Forgiveness

If you read this book all the way through and said to yourself, I just can't do it. I can't forgive them. I want you to try a few more things. My goal and objective are for you to achieve freedom when you put this book down. My prayer is that I have given you all the tools and resources that you will need to once and for all let go of the unforgiveness in your life. I hope that you apply the information and the scriptures given so that you can and will be free. Allowing the unforgiveness to stay even one more day will open you up to health-related issues in your body. That is the very reason I decided to write this book. I did not realize that holding on to issues results in physical problems and causes diseases to take up residence in your body.

To move from suffering to forgiveness, you might:

- Recognize the value of forgiveness and how it can improve your life
- Identify what needs healing, who needs to be forgiven, and what they need forgiveness
- Consider joining a support group or seeing a counselor
- Acknowledge your emotions about the harm done to you and how they affect your behavior and work to release them

Choose to forgive the person who's offended you.

Move away from your role as victim and release the control and power the offending person and situation have had in your life." I want you to understand that forgiveness is a process, and even small hurts may need to be revisited and forgiven repeatedly.

- Reflect on the times that you have hurt or disappointed someone and the fact that they forgave you.
- Ask yourself why he or she would behave in such away. Could it be that you may have reacted in the same way?
- Write in a journal. I have found that writing things out in a journal helps to process feelings and emotions.

The word works and it is true. I would not keep referring to it if it were not true. So for the next 30 days, I want to give you scriptures to help you to win this battle.

Daily Bible Verses

Day 1- I can do all things through Christ who strengthens me. Philippians 4:13

The Result: When you are going through tough times, close your eyes and envision the hosts of heaven giving you strength to be able to attack every goal and watch it happen!

Day 2- And the peace that surpasses all understanding will guard your hearts and minds in Christ Jesus. Philippians 4:6

The Result: God will give your mind the perfect peace that you need, trust Him to do it!

Day 3- "So do not fear, for I am with you; do not be dismayed, for I am your God." Isaiah 41:10

The Result: You have no need to fear! Don't be afraid of those who can kill the body: they cannot touch your soul. Gods got you and is always with you!

Day 4- And we know that all things work together for the good of those who love him and have been called according to his purpose. Romans 8:28

The Result: God said ALL THINGS. Not some things, nor a few things. He said All! Even the times when we messed up. He will circle back around and use it for our good. He truly makes all things beautiful in His time!

Day 5- For I am convinced that neither life nor death, neither angels nor demons, neither present or future, nor any powers, neither height nor depth, nor anything else in all creation, will be able to separate us from the love of God that is in Christ Jesus our Lord. Romans 8:38-39

The Result: No one, no circumstance, no situation will separate us from the Lord. The key is for us to stay close to him under the protection of His wings and watch the Lord work in our lives.

Day 6- The steadfast love of the Lord never ceases; his mercies never come to an end; they are new every morning; great is your faithfulness. Lamentations 3:22-23

The Result: God is not like man and does not hold grudges. We should strive daily to be like Him. We wake up and have a fresh batch of mercies! Let us do the same for our brothers and sisters.

Day 7- So we do not lose heart. Though our outer self is washing away, our inner self is being renewed day by day. For this light momentary affliction is preparing us for an eternal weight of glory beyond all comparison, as we look not to the things that are unseen. 2 Corinthians 4:16-18

The Result: Yes, the trial hurt and currently it feels unbearable. It certainly does not feel light by any means. The glory that will be revealed from the trial will not be compared to the trouble that you have endured. You will prevail and come out of it not even smelling like smoke.

Day 8- Greater love has no one than this; to lay down one's life for one's friends. John 15:13

The Result: Jesus died not only for our sins, but it was also so that we will be able to enter eternal life. We will be able to rule and reign with Him in eternity. The Lord is truly for us. That is the best kind of friend ever!

Day 9- Now to him who can do immeasurably more than we can ask or imagine; according to his power that is at work in us. Ephesians 3:20

The Result: What is it that you are praying for? I will go one step further, what is it that you are dreaming about. Do you know that the Lord wants you to dream even bigger than that! Your miracle will be even bigger than you can imagine! Go back and dream again!

Day 10- Be strong and courageous. Do not be afraid or terrified because of them, or the Lord your God goes with you: he will never leave you nor forsake you. Deuteronomy 31:6

The Result: Sometimes the enemy will try to make us feel small like a grasshopper. You are not that and you must walk through whatever you are facing knowing that the Lord is with you, and He's got your back. He does not have your back some of the times but, He has you always! Walk and talk like it and watch Him work!

Day 11- The Lord is my light and my salvation whom shall, I fear? The Lord is the stronghold of my life, whom shall I be afraid? Psalm 27:12.

The Result: Keeping to the theme of being strong and courageous, even afraid walk on through to the other side of the battle and I promise you that people will not see any of the scars. The only way that people will see your scars is if you show them. You will look just that good!

THE JOURNEY TO DESTINY

Day 12- There is no fear in love. But perfect love drives out fear because fear has to do with torment. The one who fears bids not made perfect in love. John 4:18

The Result- When you truly love someone, you can put your full trust in them, and you believe them. You not only believe them, but you also believe in them. When you press into loving the Lord, you will notice that your love will grow and your trust in Him will also grow. In doing that you will drive out fear from your life.

Day 13- What, then, shall we say in response to these things? If God be for us, who can be against us? Romans 8:31

The Result: You will not be liked or loved by everyone. There will be times that you may encounter some enemies even. There will be no need to worry about that. You have the most Powerful Force on the earth that is backing you. You will be victorious in the face of your enemies. Stand still and see the salvation of the Lord!

Day 14- May the God of hope fill you with all joy and peace as you trust him, so that you may overflow with hope in the power of the Holy Spirit. Romans 15:13

The Result: When was the last time that you worshiped the Lord? When you truly worship the Lord, you will feel a rush of the tangible presence of God that will bring you into a joy and peace that you will never want to leave. It is available to you today. Go to your secret place and be refreshed!

Day 15- Be strong, and let your heart take courage, all you who wait for the Lord! Psalm 31:24

The Result: Waiting on the Lord at times can be hard. It requires patience and strength so that you will not give up. The best way to combat your heart failing is to meditate on the Word of God. Find scriptures that pertain to the promise that you are waiting for to manifest. Don't just read them once or twice. You must immerse yourself in the word and then you will obtain the strength you need to carry you through!

Day 16- Fear not, for I am with you; be not dismayed, for I am your God; I will strengthen you, I will help you, I will uphold you with my righteous right hand. Isaiah 41:10

The Result: Fear Not is written in the scriptures three hundred and sixty-five times. The Lord knows that we as being human would be afraid. The Lord is so gracious and patient with us that we would keep reminding us of that fact. If you are fearful today, facing no matter what, I encourage you to seek out scriptures to bring you courage. Just a reminder, that the Lord's right hand is mighty to save!

Day 17- But they who wait on the Lord shall renew their strength; they shall mount up with wings like eagles; they shall run and not be weary; they shall walk and not faint. Isaiah 40:31

The Result: What does it mean to "Wait on the Lord?" A common meaning in most all biblical instances for waiting on the Lord is having the expectant trust and hope in God's movement and activity. God will not allow you to be ashamed who waits on Him.

Day 18- Jesus looked at them and said, "With man it is impossible, but not with God. For all things are possible with God. Mark 10:27

The Result: As humans we tend to think that when man says something, that is the final word. Not so! God is all powerful and all knowing. He knew that you would be in the position you are in before you were ever born. He is not surprised by your circumstances. Stop putting your faith in man and what they say. Allow your faith, trust and hope to be solely on the Lord. The one who is able to make ALL things possible to them that believe.

Day 19- Casting all your anxieties on him, because he cares for you. 1 Peter 5:7

The Result: What does the word casting mean? Casting means to place something on someone else. The Lord invites you to cast your burden on Him. How exactly do we do that? You pray and ask the Lord to take it and trust that He did just that. Now the big part is not to take it back. For example, if you have a wayward young adult and you are trying to control their behavior. Trust that the Lord will handle it. You still need to do your part but only God can change the heart of man. That is the Holy Spirits part not ours. We must trust him to do His part and leave the child with the Lord.

Day 20- Therefore, my beloved brothers, be steadfast, immoveable, always abounding in the work of the Lord, knowing that in the Lord your labor is not in vain. 1 Corinthians 15:58

The Result: Are you working for the Lord? Working for the Lord doesn't have to be working in the church for the Lord. Everything that we do can be done unto the Lord. Committing to do our work in excellence is one way. Having pure motives and helping people away from the public's eye is awesome but sometimes you feel that you are not getting the credit that you deserve. All these things will be rewarded in due time. The things that you do will not go wasted and it is not in vain.

Day 21- Trust in the Lord with all your heart, and do not lean on your own understanding. In all your ways acknowledge him, and he will make straight your paths. Proverbs 3:3-6

The Result: Although the stresses of daily life can quickly wear on you and make you feel overwhelmed, you're not alone in your struggles. Trusting in the Lord can offer guidance, perspective, and a sense of peace when you need it most. The Lord will make every crooked place straight for you in your life.

Day 22- "You prepare a table before me in the presence of my enemies. You anoint my head with oil; my cup overflows."

The Result: You are coming out of this battle, and everyone will see it. Not only will your loved ones see God causing your life to overflow with abundance, but your enemies will also know that you are loved by the Lord!

Day 23- For verily I say unto you, that whosoever shall say unto this mountain, be thou removed, and be thou cast into the sea; and shall not doubt in his heart but shall believe that those things which he saith shall come to pass; he shall have whatsoever he saith. Therefore, I say unto you, What things soever ye desire. When ye pray, believe ye receive them and ye shall have them.

The Result: "Say unto this mountain." The mountain equals your problem. Now when you insert your issue where the mountain is, you will receive revelation knowledge on how to believe and you will see the miracle that you need come to pass in your life. The key is to simply believe, and you will have it!

Day 24- Give thanks to the Lord for he is good: His love endures forever. Psalm 107:1

The Result- This Psalm is a Psalm of gratefulness for all that the Lord has done in our lives. Even during hard times, there is always something that we can be grateful for. Meditate on the things that are going well in your life. You may say that nothing is going right in your life. I beg to differ! You can read this book without help. You have your eyes to see! These are a few examples of how to be thankful and give thanks. God is a parent. As a parent I know how good I feel when my children show gratitude for the things that I do. The Lord is no different. He loves it! Do it today!

Day 25- "For I know the plans that I have for you," declares the Lord. plans to prosper you and not to harm you, plans to give you hope and a future. Jeremiah 29:11

The Result: The Lord has great plans for you. Through your struggles, great purpose will come out of your life. Feel confident today that you are loved and cared for even before the foundation of the world. Your future is bright, but you must see it, before you see it. All in your mind's eye!

Day 26- Taste and see that the Lord is good; blessed is the one who takes refuge in him. Psalm 34:8

The Result: At times like these we can see the goodness of God and put our trust in Him. When we put our trust in the Lord, we will be closer to Him. His desire for us is to have peace. This all comes down to trust in the maker of Heaven and Earth.

Day 27- To the person who pleases Him, God gives wisdom, knowledge, and happiness, but to the sinner he gives the task of gathering and storing up wealth to hand over to the one that pleases God. This too is meaningless, chasing after the wind. Ecclesiastes 2:26

The Result: There are times when you are serving the Lord and nothing in your life is going right. However, your unsaved acquaintance's life has nothing but great things happening, and they don't serve your God or even like your God. It can feel very painful, and you ask yourself why you even bother! This message is for you! Hold on a little while longer because the wealth of the sinner is about to be transferred to the righteous. Just make sure that you are the righteous!

Day 28- "For His anger is but for a moment, His favor is for life: weeping may endure for a night, but joy comes in the morning." Psalm 30:5

The Result: Have you ever noticed that problems feel the worst in the midnight hour? That is when the enemy of your soul can torment you the most. I can attest to this personally. You cry and cry and you think that the trouble will never end. Then you fall asleep, and you wake up in the morning and things feel a little better. I challenge you to know that each day you are one step closer to your blessing. Wipe your tears because joy is truly coming.

Day 29- Take delight in the Lord, and he will give you the desires of your heart. Psalm 37:4

The Result: The "desires of your heart" are those secret things that you have never told anyone about. The dreams are big and small. Even your small dreams greatly matter to the Lord, and He wants to give them to you. Simply delight in the Lord. You ask, "How do I do that?" To delight yourself in the Lord you must first have a relationship with Him. He wants you to know him. Have walks and talks with him to establish intimacy. He wants you to know Him as your Father and your friend.

Day 30- "Those who sow in tears shall reap in joy." Psalm 126:5

The Result: We must remember to look ahead in our struggles. The suffering and challenges we gave today will turn into joy. The tears that we shed today will be like seeds that are planted in a field that in time through much toil and suffering will rise to a great harvest of joy and thankfulness.

ACKNOWLEDGMENTS

Thank you, Dr. Sherrie Walton (Walton Publishing House), for your guidance, patience & prayers.

I want to thank my family and friends for their encouragement to write the book.

Finally, I would like to thank God for the strength and the ability to be able to encourage His children.

ABOUT THE AUTHOR

Sheila R. Smith is the founder of Fresh Fire International Ministries Inc, a 501c3 that assists underserved communities with food, clothing, and counseling services. Sheila is a licensed Minister of the Gospel of Jesus Christ for 20 years and a life coach. Through the school of hard knocks and life's trials and tribulations, she has more than 30 years of walking people through the worst seasons of their lives and getting them past their pain.

Sheila has 25+ years' experience of recognized performance excellence in operations, retail, customer care, employee retention, and mentorship. She is a highly motivated and driven General Manager/Human Resource Manager and is successful at implementing strategic approaches to drive profitability and sales with a strong ability to drive profits, control costs, and achieve continuous process improvement.

Ms. Smith is also an expert authority on research and trend identification and human resources management developments combined with extensive project plans, data integration that has worked independently or collaboratively to continue to develop and explore alternative HRM solutions and presents new or modified programs to executive leadership.

Sheila is a mother of 4 adult children and 14 grandchildren along and recently married to her husband Dennis.

.

Made in the USA
Columbia, SC
19 July 2022

63669322R00085